FABER & FABER

3 QUEEN SQUARE
LONDON

Table Tennis

Harold Myers

In the same series
JUDO
by George Glass
RALLYING
by Chris Sclater &
Martin Holmes

First published in 1977 by Faber and Faber Limited
3 Queen Square London WC1N 3AU
Set by Filmtype Services Limited
Printed in Great Britain by
The Riverside Press Ltd., London and Whitstable
All Rights Reserved
© Harold Myers 1977

ACKNOWLEDGEMENTS

The author and publishers would like to thank
Mike Johns and Carol Johnson, who acted as
models for the photographs, John Mills
Photography Ltd, Liverpool, for producing the
photographs, and May Kelly and Ron Graham for
their help in preparing the manuscript.
Photographs on the title page, contents and
introduction by A. C. Coombs, A.I.I.P.

British Library Cataloguing in Publication Data

Myers, Harold
    Table tennis.
    1. Table tennis – Handbooks, manuals, etc.
    I. Title
    796.34'6   GV1005

ISBN 0-571-11001-0

Contents

Foreword

Having worked with Harold Myers on many occasions, I am quite familiar with his methods of coaching, and in this book he has clearly illustrated all the basic strokes of table tennis and set out a very comprehensive range of progressive training exercises which I feel would be most useful for all players, from the beginner to the advanced player.

Denis Neale

Five Times Champion of England

Table tennis is now one of our most popular sports, possibly because players of all ages can participate in a game which can be played all the year round in almost any room which is large enough to take a table tennis table.

Of course there are certain conditions laid down for competitive match play, which vary according to the level of competition. But whatever the conditions and whatever the level of play, everybody can enjoy one of the most popular sports in the world.

With this in mind, this book aims to help all, from the raw beginner to the top-class player, to improve their game.

Table Tennis News

For up-to-date information on events, rules and personalities there is nothing better than the magazine of the English Table Tennis Association. It is published monthly and can be obtained from their headquarters – E.T.T.A. 21 Claremont, Hastings, East Sussex.

1 *Preparation for playing*

THE BEGINNER

A question often asked of me is – 'at what age should you start to play table tennis?' – and the answer is really quite simple. You can begin to play at any age between seven and seventy years old, but although the training would be basically the same, the application may differ according to age, height, weight, physique, etc.

CHOOSING A BAT

The first thing you must decide is which bat to use, and since this is the most important piece of table tennis equipment you will possess, it is important to take special care when purchasing a bat.

It is difficult to generalize about bats because there are so many varieties, but I think the main consideration should be that the bat *feels* comfortable in the hand and the weight is neither too heavy nor too light. In fact the bat should be, as far as possible, a natural extension of the hand.

You must also consider the covering on the blade of the bat, and this usually causes quite a problem to the beginner. Since he cannot as yet play the game and so at this stage does not know which type of player he will be, how can he possibly decide which of the many rubbers available would be most suitable for him? As a guide line, I would recommend that the beginner choose a 'reversed sponge' bat of medium speed and spin qualities. When buying such a bat make sure you read the manufacturer's specifications, usually found on the reverse of the box and *always* insist on holding the bat to see if it 'feels right' in your hand. As your game improves you will probably change your bat regularly (bats don't last for ever) and by this time you will have had enough experience to know exactly which type of bat is best for your particular style of play.

THE GRIP

There are really only two ways to hold the bat: the WESTERN GRIP (often referred to as the SHAKE HANDS GRIP) and the PEN-HOLD GRIP, used mainly by Asian players. Whichever grip you use, remember that the most important thing is that the bat should fit comfortably in the hand and that it also *feels* right.

The first six photographs illustrate the easiest way to find the correct grip.

The Western grip

Hold the bat, by the blade, in the non-playing hand.

Place three fingers around the handle of the bat, with the thumb resting along the edge of the blade near the handle. This side of the bat is referred to as the FOREHAND.

This photograph shows the other side of the bat, with the index finger lying along the edge of the blade near the handle. This side of the bat is known as the BACKHAND.

Since the penhold grip allows only for the use of one side of the bat, it follows that the player using this grip must adapt his style of play accordingly, although the basic stroke play is virtually the same for both the Penholder and the Western-style player.

However, in this book it is assumed that the player will adopt the Western grip and thus all strokes etc. will be demonstrated using it.

The Penhold grip

Take hold of the bat, by the blade, in the non-playing hand.

Grip the handle as if holding a pencil, with the thumb and index finger almost meeting on the playing surface of the bat.

The three other fingers give support on the non-playing surface of the bat.

So now we're ready to start – or are we?

You have a bat and you know how to hold it, but before you dash off to the nearest sports centre to try out your new bat, let me remind you of the other equipment you will need.

Starting from the feet, you will need a pair of sports shoes, and, as a matching set, nothing looks neater than white ankle socks. Then there's the shorts or skirt – remember to choose a dark colour to conform to regulations when you eventually reach competitive match play. Finally, a short-sleeved sports shirt adds the finishing touch to the 'complete player', and here again a plain, dark-coloured shirt is advisable. A track suit is not essential, but you should have a thick pullover or cardigan with you so that you can keep warm in between practices or games.

I don't want to give the impression that all these 'extra' items are absolutely necessary to play table tennis – after all, it is a leisure activity which can be played almost anywhere – but my reasons for suggesting the purchase of regulation kit are twofold.

First, from a hygienic point of view, it is surely better to have a change of clothing after any physical activity.

Second, a player who 'looks the part' will psychologically have an advantage over the player who turns up for a match or practice session in hobnailed boots and overalls!

If you take this thought a little further, would you go swimming in football kit? Or would you play football in cricket gear? Of course you wouldn't, because every sport has its own playing kit, and table tennis is no exception – so try your best to look correct. Then you will feel much more the part and therefore play better.

POSITIONING

In all strokes, both simple and advanced, positioning is of vital importance, and the following illustrations show the basic 'ready' positions.

Central ready stance

Front view

Side view

The weight is balanced on the balls of the feet which are roughly shoulder-width apart. The knees are flexed and pointing slightly inward. The forearm of the playing arm is in a horizontal position while the upper arm is vertical. The whole body is leaning forward slightly and is positioned about an arm's-length away from the table.

This stance should be used when receiving services, and will enable you to move quickly in any direction and thus position yourself to make a good return, using either forehand or backhand.

Side view

Front view

Positioning for backhand strokes

For backhand strokes played near to the table, there is only a small deviation from the central stance, in as much as the right foot is leading slightly.

When playing backhand strokes away from the table (in particular backhand defensive strokes) the body is positioned with the right shoulder pointing toward the net and the right foot is further advanced.

Positioning for forehand strokes

When playing forehand strokes, the body should be positioned with the left shoulder nearer to the net and the left foot leading.

Side view

Front view

In certain positions, such as the two shots shown below, it is easier to reverse the 'standard' position of the feet.

Short backhand

Short forehand

Remember, whichever stance you use, the main principles are: good balance, flexibility of knees, lightness on the feet – but most of all, make sure you get in a position to play the ball, even if it means using 'incorrect' footwork or positioning.

3 Basic stroke production 2

The first basic stroke to master is the PUSH STROKE, and acquiring a good push shot is essential in the early stages of play, since this stroke is the basis for so many other strokes which you will learn as you progress.

Each stroke in table tennis can be analysed into three simple sections.

1 Preparation for the stroke to be played, and the STARTING POSITION of the bat.

2 Movement of the bat from the starting position to the CONTACT POSITION – this stage of the stroke would include subtle changes in the angle of the bat and the TIMING of the contact between bat and ball.

3 The FOLLOW-THROUGH, which is the movement made after striking the ball, is important because to some extent it controls the balance of the player and also has a strong bearing on the power and speed of the shot produced.

Each section, however, has many variations which will all have to be mastered in due course, but initially the important thing is to know how to produce the 'mean' (i.e. average) stroke.

A brief explanation of TIMING is necessary before we move on to the first stroke.

Timing is directly related to the position of contact between bat and ball, as the diagram shows:

flight path of ball →

A: Just after the bounce – EARLY

B: Top height after the bounce – PEAK

C: Late in the ball's descent – LATE

D: Very late in the descent stage – VERY LATE

The four points A B C D are just a simple illustration of the main timing points used throughout this book, but in actual fact the ball can be struck at *any* point between A and D, depending on the position of the player and type of stroke played.

Ladies can play too

Although I refer throughout the book to a male player, I don't want to give you the impression that this is a 'men only' sport – indeed there are a great number of women playing table tennis in all parts of the world. So with due apologies to any female reader, we can now proceed to study our first steps in stroke play.

Backhand push

Starting position
The arm is drawn close into the body. Bat angle is 'open'. Right foot is advanced with weight on the left leg.

Arm movement

Positioning of feet

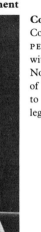

Contact
Contact is made about PEAK of bounce, still with open bat angle. Notice how the weight of the body has begun to transfer from back leg to front leg.

Follow-through
Arm follows through straight after contact. Open angle of bat at this stage is more accentuated. Weight is now fully transferred to front foot.

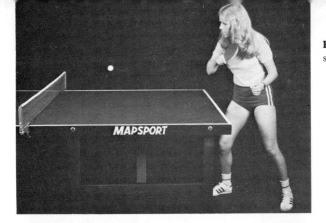

Backhand push
seen from the side

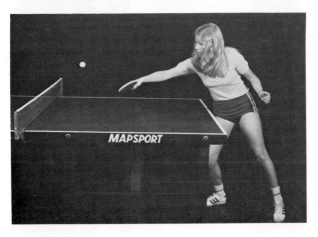

Forehand push

Starting position

Be sure to start the stroke with the arm clear of the body. Left shoulder is turned toward the net. Open bat angle. Left leg is advanced with weight on right leg.

Contact

Contact is made at the top of the bounce with bat angle still open. Notice how right shoulder is 'dropping' as weight is gradually being transferred to front foot.

Follow-through

Arm follows through almost straight, and right shoulder is in a low position as weight is now transferred to front leg.

Forehand push
seen from the side.

23

ATTACKING STROKES

Every player in the early stages of progress has an urge to hit the ball hard and fast, just like the top players in the game, and I think that once the basic 'touch' strokes have been learned, the next stage is ATTACK.

The first 'aggressive' stroke to attempt is the FLAT HIT.

The flat hit would be used to drive a ball which has been returned fairly high by your opponent with very little spin.

Forehand flat hit

Starting position
Notice similar stance to forehand push, but this time the bat angle is vertical or slightly closed and the bat is held lower. The right hip is rotated away from the table.

Contact
Ball is struck at the top of the bounce with the bat angle now closed a little. Right hip and

shoulder now turning toward the net as contact is made.

Follow-through
Bat continues in a forward motion after contact. Weight of body fully transferred forward. Short follow-through enables the striker to regain position for the next shot.

Backhand flat hit

There is very little difference between the backhand and forehand flat hit, but you should remember that, as a general rule, backhand strokes over or near to the end of the table require a lesser degree of body movement than does the comparable forehand stroke.

Starting position
Striking arm is held fairly low, but is elevated to the height of the oncoming ball before contact is made. The right foot is advanced.

Contact
Full contact is made between bat and ball, with the bat striking 'through' the ball.

Follow-through
The arm is fully extended after contact and the body weight is now concentrated on the front foot.

THE BLOCKING STROKE

In order to practise your strokes, it is
essential to have a sparring partner with you,
who can 'feed' each ball accurately to your
court. The CONTROLLER (this is the name
we give to your feeder) does not *have* to be a
top-class player – in fact two beginners
can work together quite well, by taking turns
to act as the controller, but herein lies a
problem. Initially you could both return the
'pushed' ball, because both the PLAYER and
the CONTROLLER were using the same type
of stroke. But now that you have advanced to
hitting the ball reasonably hard, it leaves the
receiving player stranded somewhat, because
he has not yet learned how to deal with the
quicker-played ball. So now I'm hoping to
give you a solution to this problem by
showing you the easiest way to return a fast
moving ball – the blocking stroke.

There are two main blocking shots used in
general play.
   The first of these is the REFLECTIVE
BLOCK which can be described simply as
allowing the oncoming ball to strike the bat
and rebound along the same line of play.
   Second, by altering the horizontal angle
of the bat, the oncoming ball can be projected to a different direction from the
original flight-path – this is known for
obvious reasons as the DEFLECTIVE BLOCK.
   All blocking strokes have one thing in
common: the angle of the bat, on contact,
must be accurately adjusted for each ball
played.
   Later on in the book, we'll be dealing with
topspin, and since the block shot is probably
the one most commonly used to return topspin, keep in mind what I have written about
'accurately adjusting the bat angles'.

The reflective block

Starting position
Fairly square position with bat held near to the table surface.

Backhand

Forehand

Contact
The oncoming ball is played 'early' (just after the bounce) with vertical to closed angle bat.

Follow-through
There is virtually no follow-through since the object of this stroke is simply to let the ball rebound back over the net.

The deflective block

The *deflective* blocking stroke differs from the *reflective* blocking stroke in one respect only. The horizontal angle of the bat, on contact, is adjusted to deflect the oncoming ball to the desired position on the opponent's half of the table.

Backhand   **Forehand**

I think most people realize that any spherical object can be made to spin, and a table tennis ball is no exception. The majority of shots in table tennis employ spin of one kind or another in varying degrees of rotation. The three types of spin are:

4 *Spin*

1 TOPSPIN: used mainly as an attacking stroke
2 BACKSPIN: often referred to as 'under-spin' or 'chop', and used for defensive play
3 SIDESPIN: combined with either topspin or backspin, has the effect of making the ball swerve sideways in flight

Topspin

Topsin is effected by the forward and up-ward 'brushing' action of the bat on the ball, and there are two basic methods of achieving this type of spin:

1 by moving the arm in an upward plane

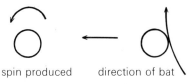

spin produced   direction of bat

and
2 by moving the arm in a forward and upward direction.

spin produced   direction of bat

In both cases the effect is to make the ball rotate in a forward direction, the effects of which are as follows:

The ball in flight will tend to dip suddenly, and on landing will 'kick off' at a low angle

and consequently on contact with the receiver's bat will tend to shoot up sharply.

Backspin

As the name suggests, the object here is to make the forward-moving ball rotate backwards, toward the striker, and this is achieved by moving the bat in a downward direction and 'cutting' under the ball with an open-angled bat.

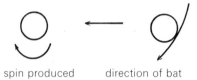

spin produced   direction of bat

The ball with backspin imparted tends to soar in flight, and on landing, the braking effect of the backspin induces the ball to spin back toward the net, particularly so after contact with the receiver's bat.

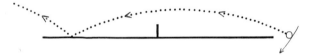

Sidespin

Sidespin is usually accompanied by either topspin or backspin, but the general effect of sidespin is to make the ball swerve in flight and deflect sideways on contact with the table surface.

Sidespin is achieved by drawing the bat around the ball and the application of either an upward or downward action will determine the additional topspin or backspin effect.

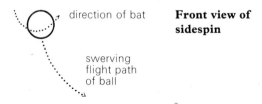

direction of bat   **Front view of
sidespin**

swerving
flight path
of ball

The degree and speed of the spin imparted can and should be varied by altering the angle of the bat, the contact position on the ball and the emphasis of the arm and body movement.

As a general rule, the slighter the contact between bat and ball, the greater will be the spin imparted, and, conversely, heavier or fuller contact will produce less spin.

There are so many spin variations that it is quite impossible to detail every one, but it is nevertheless important to practise and experiment with spin so that eventually you will become aware of your own limitations in using spin tactically and effectively.

5 *Services*

So far you have studied the basic strokes, and you now have some idea of what is meant by spin. It is at this stage that I shall deal with serving.

It may seem a little out of order to bring in services *after* learning the basic strokes, but from experience I have found that the beginner is more able to cope with service actions after he has gained a little experience of touch control, ball sense, co-ordination, etc.

Before detailing the various services we must be sure of the Rules governing serving, for it is no use having an elaborate service if it doesn't comply with the Rules.

The main points in the *Laws of the Game* concerning serving are:

The ball should be placed on the flat palm of the free hand, which must be stationary with the fingers together and the thumb free. The ball should then be projected upward, as near vertical as possible, so as to be visible by the umpire at all times.

The ball is then struck as it is descending from the height of its trajectory, so that it first touches the server's court and then passes directly over or around the net and its supports and touches the receiver's court.

When serving, the ball must be struck above the height of the playing surface of the table and behind the base line (end) of the table.

Should the ball touch the net or its supports in passing from one court to the other, a 'let' is called, and the service must be re-taken.

Note A more detailed section of the main rules of the game (extracted from the official *Laws of the International Table Tennis Federation*) can be found at the end of this book.

The following photographs show a variety of services, but it is up to you to experiment and find your own personal best service. The start (1), contact (2) and follow-through (3) positions are shown for each service.

Backspin service   **Main features:** The bat 'cuts' the ball in a downward action with an open-angled bat.

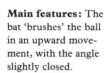

Main features: The bat 'brushes' the ball in an upward movement, with the angle slightly closed.

Topspin service

Topspin with sidespin (*Left*)

Main features: The bat brushes upward and 'drags' across the surface of the ball.

Backspin with sidespin (*Right*)

Main features: The bat cuts down and 'drags' round the ball.

Practise all the service variations on both backhand and forehand and invent your own 'special' services. And remember to try to direct each service to every part of your opponent's court, playing some short (just over the net) and others long (near to the far end of the table).

6 Topspin attacking strokes

There are several ways in which a ball can be returned using topspin, but the deciding factor must be the evaluation of the arriving ball. You must observe your opponent from the beginning of his stroke to determine which type of ball he is returning to you, so that you in turn can decide exactly which stroke to play in order to make a safe return.

Points to watch for are:

1 His stance – is he 'shaping up' to play a backspin stroke, or perhaps a blocked return, etc.?

2 His arm action will in most cases indicate most definitely which type of spin he is employing. But watch out for the clever, more experienced player who can disguise his action and thus fool you into treating his return incorrectly.

3 Be aware of your own position in relation to the oncoming ball, and decide before the ball arrives whether or not your position will limit you in any way in choosing any particular stroke to make the return.

All these points will come with experience, but I feel it should be part of your initial training to be aware of your opponent, even if he is at this stage only a sparring partner.

The topspin stroke has to be modified depending on the type of ball received. For instance, playing a topspin shot against blocked returns is different from a topspin shot against defensively 'chopped' balls, and similarly if your opponent plays topspin to you, you must alter your stroke accordingly in order to return the ball with topspin.

So it can be seen that there are many different strokes, all under the heading of topspin, and I can only endeavour to enlighten you on the main general principles of evaluation and execution of the stroke.

TOPSPIN AGAINST A BLOCKED RETURN –
over the table

Forehand

Starting position
The bat is held at table height with the right hip partially turned away from the net. The bat angle is closed.

Contact
The bat moves forward and upward striking the ball along the top surface. Contact is made when the ball is in the 'peak' position of the bounce.

Follow-through
The hips are rotated in the same direction as the bat. The follow-through is quite short and the weight is now fully transferred to the front leg.

Backhand

Starting position
Bat held at table height.
Fairly square stance.

Contact
The closed-angled bat
is 'rolled' over the top
surface of the ball. The
ball is struck at the top
of the bounce.

Follow-through
Arm is almost straight,
with a slight but
noticeable 'turn-over'
of the wrist.

The following photographs show the same strokes played against a blocked return when the striker is positioned away from the table, which necessitates a modification of the stroke, since the ball is contacted later in the bounce.

Forehand

Starting position
Weight on back leg, with knees flexed and hips rotated away from the net.

Contact
The ball is struck during its descent from the 'peak' position.

Follow-through
Hips move in a forward, 'spiralling' manner, transferring the weight of the body to the front foot.

Backhand

Starting position
Knees bent with body in a 'squat' position. Bat starts in a low position.

Contact
Arm moves in an upward arc. The bat strikes the ball during its descent from the peak position.

Follow-through
Weight is transferred forward and upward as bat follows through fairly high after contact.

MAPSPORT

TOPSPIN AGAINST BACKSPIN RETURNS

Forehand

Starting position
The bat starts in a low position with a closed angle. Weight is on the back leg.

Contact
Contact is made when the ball is in the 'late' position of the bounce, thus allowing some of the backspin on the ball to die out.

Follow-through
Notice the long, high arm action. The weight is now on the front leg.

Backhand

Starting position
Position of body is fairly square to the flight-path of the on-coming ball. The bat is held in a low position.

Contact
'Late' contact on the ball with a closed-angled bat.

Follow-through
High follow-through with weight of the body transferred more 'upward' than forward.

These diagrams may help you to understand
the timing differences between the various
strokes.

**Topspin against a block return –
Played near to the table**

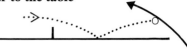

**As above but played away from the
table**

Topspin against 'chopped' returns

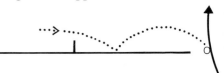

These illustrations should only be considered as guidelines, and in no way do they
cover the entire range of variations of contact
positions and arm movements.

Players of different stature must adapt
their method of stroke play to suit their own
personal physique. In other words a tall
player with long arms could achieve the
same results by playing a slightly different
stroke from that of a small player with short
arms.

The contact point would also alter according to the distance from the table, at which
the player is positioned. The nearer the
table, the earlier the contact point; conversely, a later contact would be made as the
player moves further away from the table.

TOPSPIN LOOPED DRIVE

In the modern game of table tennis the 'loop' is often regarded as some kind of wonder shot, but in actual fact a 'looped drive' is simply an exaggerated form of top-spin and should be thought of as such. However, the extra spin achieved by looping the ball could cause problems for your opponent and thus win a point for you, so it is important to know how to convert your *ordinary* topspin drive into a *looped* topspin drive.

In the main, a looped drive is used against backspin returns, although there is no reason whatsoever why the same stroke cannot be applied to any type of ball received, provided the player makes the necessary adjustments to the arm movement and contact point.

THE LOOPED DRIVE AGAINST A BACKSPIN RETURN

Forehand

Starting position
The bat is held very low and almost behind the body. The right hip is turned away from the net with body weight low on the back leg. The angle of the bat is closed slightly at the start of the stroke.

Contact position
Quite a late contact point, with bat angle now noticeably vertical/open. Just at the point of contact there is a definite flick of the wrist, which in itself imparts more topspin to the ball.

Follow-through
The bat follows through fairly high with the body weight transferred upward in a spiralling movement.

THE LOOPED DRIVE AGAINST CHOPPED RETURNS

Backhand

Starting position
Notice the almost
square stance, with
the bat held very low.
The knees are bent
with the weight of the
body bearing down on
the feet.

Contact position
Ball is struck when it is
in a 'late' position after
the bounce. The bat
angle is now vertical/open,
and again there
is a sharp wrist flick
just at the moment
of contact.

Follow-through
The follow-through is
high and the weight
follows the path of the
bat in an upward
movement.

It is quite possible to play a looped drive while taking the ball at a fairly high point of contact but in this case the arm action must be adjusted to compensate for the variance in the stroke production.

Once again, I must emphasize that the looped drive is quite an advanced stroke and requires much practice to perfect, and in particular the player has to develop a smooth fast stroke while at the same time he must learn to time his stroke and to adjust the bat angle so that the bat makes a minimum of contact with the ball to ensure a resulting fast forward spin.

As I have mentioned previously, looping is not the 'be all and end all' of table tennis and my own view is that the ability to play an *effective* looped drive depends to some extent on the physical structure of the individual player, and one must always take this into consideration.

Whenever you have the opportunity to watch top international players, study their various styles and methods of looping and afterwards you may come to the conclusion that there isn't really a *specific* looped drive as such – and you would be quite correct!

The main thing in common with all these various loops, is the exaggerated amount of topspin imparted on the ball. It is up to you to find the easiest way to achieve this type of spin, following the basic lines of movement shown in the photographs.

Note I would suggest that beginners should acquire a reasonably good topspin drive before attempting the more advanced 'looped' drive.

The easiest way to describe backspin defensive strokes (sometimes referred to as 'chopped' returns) is to compare the stroke with the basic push shot.

By comparing the next set of photographs with the earlier illustrations of the push strokes, you will see that the backspin defensive stroke is more or less an extension of the push, but employing a longer arm action.

Backspin strokes are used mainly to return topspin balls, and here again it is important to realize that the amount of backspin imparted to the ball can be varied by the severity of the cutting action of the bat on the ball.

Even the all-out attacking player should master backspin defensive strokes, not only because it is an aspect of the game which the good all-round player needs as part of his wide scope of stroke production, but more importantly, he can also gain a tactical advantage by slipping in a 'chop', and in doing so may break his opponent's concentration by the unexpected change of pace and spin.

Once again the degree of spin on the ball can be varied by the lightness of the contact between bat and ball, and also the point on the ball where the bat strikes it.

For example :

A Only a small amount of backspin applied
B More backspin imparted
C Severe backspin

X indicates the point where the bat strikes the ball

7 *Backspin defensive strokes*

Forehand

Starting position
The bat is held about shoulder height. The left leg is advanced with the weight on the back leg.

Contact position
The bat moves in a downward cutting action making contact when the ball is in a 'late' position after the bounce. The angle of the bat is open on contact.

Follow-through
The follow-through is shallow and low. The weight is transferred downward.

Backhand

Starting position
Open-angled bat –
start between waist and
shoulder. The weight
at the start of the stroke
is on the back leg.

Contact position
The knees are bent as
the weight moves
downward. Fairly late
contact on ball with
the bat angle open.

Follow-through
The follow-through is
quite shallow.

8 *Spin combinations*

SIDESPIN WITH TOPSPIN

A more effective way of playing a topspin drive is to add an element of sidespin to the ball, since the combined effect of the two spins gives your opponent a double problem to deal with.

In the main, sidespin with topspin is performed more accurately with the forehand, and is not really suitable for backhand play where the twisting movement required of the body while on the move would be somewhat limited; but this is not particularly evident when serving from a stationary position.

SIDESPIN WITH BACKSPIN

It is *possible* to combine sidespin with backspin, but this is fairly uncommon since the overall effect does not present too much of a problem for your opponent.

The main uses of sidespin with backspin are when pushing, particularly on the backhand (since the arm movement required is less restricted on the backhand than it is on the forehand), and when making a 'chopped smash' as described in the following pages.

Don't forget, however, that serving lends itself to all combinations of spin and every player should make experiments.

SIDESPIN WITH TOPSPIN DRIVE

Forehand

Starting position
The angle of the bat is closed at the beginning of the stroke. The hips are rotated away from the net in a low position. Notice that the bat is in a low position at the start of the action.

Contact
Still with a closed-angled bat the arm moves in an arc, dragging round the ball on contact.

Follow-through
The bat continues to move in a sideways and upward arc, the hips following in a similar movement until the body weight is transferred to the front foot.

THE SIDESPIN CHOPPED SMASH

This particular shot can be used as a means of 'killing' outright a ball which has been returned very high by your opponent.

When executed correctly, it is a very effective way of winning the point because, as the ball touches your opponent's court, not only is it travelling very fast, but also the sidespin has the effect of making it 'kick' off the table at an awkward high angle, and since there is still a strong element of back-spin on the ball your opponent will have great difficulty in making a safe return – assuming that he can in the first instance get his bat to the ball.

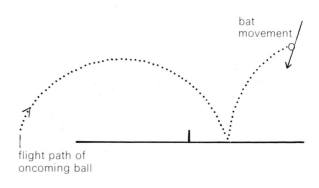

bat
movement

flight path of
oncoming ball

Starting position
Bat held very high
with the angle open.

Contact
The ball is taken at the
top of the bounce and
struck with a severe
downward and side-
ways action.

N.B. The contact point
may be varied depend-
ing on the height the
ball reaches after the
bounce and the physical
height of the player.

Follow-through
The bat travels directly
downward and side-
ways to the table
surface. Care must be
taken to avoid hitting
the table with the bat,
which would almost
inevitably result in a
damaged bat.

COUNTER HITTING

As a spectator at a top level match, one could be forgiven for thinking that the only significant stroke used is the counter driving shot, but you should bear in mind that the reason for this is probably that the players battling it out haven't got time to make a refined stroke because the ball is travelling at an extremely fast speed, and consequently if both players are positioned near to the end of the table a short fast stroke is necessary to return the ball safely.

Forehand

Starting position
The stance is almost square to the line of play, with the bat held 'at the ready'.

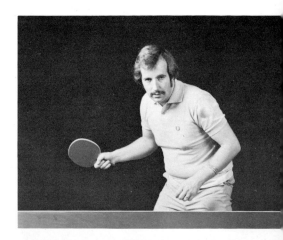

Contact
A short arm movement is all that is required, striking the ball with a closed-angled bat.

I have omitted to show the follow-through positions since there is very little movement after contact is made, the main point being that the bat must move very quickly back to the 'ready' position after striking the ball, in preparation for the next shot.

Backhand

Starting position
Square stance with knees flexed, with bat 'ready' in front of the body.

Contact
The forearm and wrist make most of the movement, bringing the bat to contact the ball at the peak of the bounce.

TOPSPIN DEFENSIVE RETURNS

Many players often find themselves driven back from the table by their opponent's powerful hitting and, as a possible means of returning the ball safely, a topspin defensive stroke is often used: but be warned – a badly placed defensive 'lob' can give your opponent an easy chance to win the point.

When playing the 'lobbed' topspin defensive return it is important to play the ball high over the net and at the same time to gauge the strength of the stroke so that the ball lands near to the baseline of your opponent's half of the table, thus making it more difficult for him to execute his next 'kill'.

The more topspin you can put on the ball, the harder it will be for your opponent to return it, so you must try to combine the three main ingredients of this stroke – topspin, height and length.

Similar to the method described opposite, the topspin lob can be played equally well with the backhand.

Starting position
The action starts with the bat held in a fairly low position.

Contact
Bat is moved forward and upward, contacting the ball late. The angle of the bat can be varied to alter the spin and trajectory of the ball.

Follow-through
The arm continues in an upward plane after contact.

THE DROP SHOT

Following on from the last stroke, it is
obvious that nothing can be gained by contin-
ually hitting the ball with every ounce
of strength you possess if your opponent is
effectively returning the ball every time. So
now we must consider a way of breaking up
his control in order to win the point.

In most cases the defensive player positions himself a long way from the table, and
this in itself should give you a clue as to how
you can deal with the situation.

One very effective method of 'destroying'
a defender is to 'drop' the ball short over
the net so that he has to move a long way
forward to play his next return. Even if he
returns the 'dropped' ball successfully, he is
then in a position over the table and the
alert attacker can take advantage of this by
hitting the ball hard and fast to force his
opponent into making a mistake. But be
careful: a too high drop shot will present the
defender with an easy 'kill'.

An effective drop shot requires no particular preparation as such, since the essence of
such a stroke is the element of surprise;
therefore it will suffice to illustrate only the
basic movements.

Against backspin defensive returns

Contact point
The bat angle is very open, making contact with the ball early after the bounce. The arm moves in a short forward movement and at the exact moment of contact the bat is drawn sharply away from the ball, thus creating a 'deadening' effect on the oncoming ball.

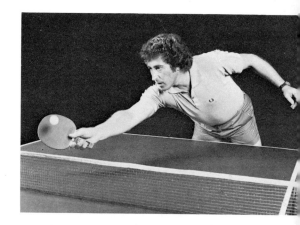

Against topspin defensive returns

Contact point
The only difference here is the angle of the bat which is closed.

9 *Tactics*

It would be a mammoth task to detail all the various permutations of possible tactical points in competitive match play, since every player has his own style of play and level of mental and physical alertness, coupled with many personal weaknesses. This being so, I can only endeavour to point out the general aspects of match-winning tactical points.

1 *Know your own limitations*
Try to analyse your own faults, and of course work hard to correct them.

2 *Observe your opponent at all times*
By watching your opponent in play (even before a match if possible) you can very often find his weakness and accordingly adjust your own game, if necessary, to play on his shortcomings.

3 *Be aware of your own mistakes*
If you can assess the faults in your game, by which your opponent is winning points, you will at least have a chance to remedy the situation.

4 *Keep your opponent on the move*
By varying the length, direction, speed and spin of the ball you will be able to make your opponent change positions and strokes constantly, the likely result being either a forced or unforced error on his part.

5 *Don't lose your temper*
Keep cool during a game, no matter how much you may be provoked. A player who cannot control his own mind has little chance of controlling a small, fast-moving table tennis ball. As an after-thought, don't go 'off at the deep end' after the game either; not only will it do you no good whatsoever, but it will mark you as a bad sportsman.

6 *Be in control of the situation*
In order to dictate the game you must learn to keep calm and allow your brain to think clearly and effectively.

7 *Keep fit*
Last, but by no means least, a fast-moving game like table tennis requires a high degree of physical fitness. It is entirely up to you to train for this!

10 *Training practices*

Now that you have acquired a basic knowledge and understanding of stroke play, it is essential for you to practise. This section of the book sets out a full range of training exercises, and by dedicating yourself to covering the full programme systematically you will certainly improve your standard of play. The exercises have been divided into four sections, each one dealing with a specific aspect of the game.

Section one covers all the basic strokes and is designed to give the player practice in consistency, accuracy, control and mobility.

The second section illustrates various exercises to combine all the strokes, and concentrates mainly on positional changes, accuracy and mobility.

The third section sets out a progressive programme incorporating all the recognized stages of training up to the nearest one can get to actual match play.

The fourth section is intended for use in schools and clubs, where normally several players would want to practise at the same time on one table.

Serving and receiving services is a most important part of the game, but since there are no specific exercises to improve this aspect of play, I would advise all players to practise serving to all parts of the table using as many different services as possible. Don't be afraid to try new services (in practice) since by experiment you may discover a new 'deadly weapon'.

So get yourself a partner and you're ready to start!

A player of your own standard is quite suitable, because the exercises are designed so that the controller's task is sufficiently easy for him to feed the ball to you correctly. Change places with your partner (the controller) at regular intervals, so that you gain experience as the controller as well as the player – this will give you a double benefit from each exercise.

NOTES ON
THE EXERCISES

The lines on the diagrams indicate the path of the player's ball only, and the letters in the text beneath each diagram correspond to the table sections as shown on the next page. The letters indicate a specific area of the table and players should endeavour to place the ball as accurately as possible within the box covered by the letter.

The easiest way to define the target areas visually on the table is to use small adhesive tabs – these will not impair the playing surface if they are *lightly* pressed on to the table.

The controller's task is illustrated in words only, and you will notice that in most cases the controller has a choice in the use of forehand or backhand returns. The reason for this is that the controller's task is simply to return the ball to the targets indicated at the correct speed and with the right amount of spin, and consequently the controller can choose either forehand or backhand, depending on which is his stronger and more accurate stroke.

Most of the exercises are described step by step, starting with the opening service from the controller. When the last numbered stroke in the sequence is reached, the rally is continued by repeating all the movements from stage number 2.

When practising, a target number should be set. For instance, inexperienced players should initially try to play ten good balls without error, and gradually increase this target up to fifty. To keep a note of progress, mark off the completed target number on the panel at the foot of each exercise.

Where more than one stroke is specified in an exercise, each completed circuit is counted as one point toward your 'target achieved'.

It isn't necessary to work systematically through the exercises in the order in which they are written. The best way is to try two or three exercises for one specific stroke, then move on to another stroke, provided that you *always* mark your 'target achieved' after each practice so that you can go back later to any particular exercise where you were not able to achieve a maximum target number.

TABLE SECTIONS

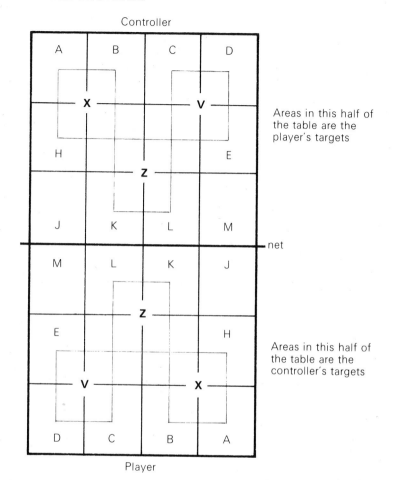

Controller

Areas in this half of the table are the player's targets

net

Areas in this half of the table are the controller's targets

Player

ABBREVIATIONS USED IN THE EXERCISES

F.H. Forehand
B.H. Backhand
T/S Topspin
B/S. Backspin (or chop)
S/S Sidespin
C Controller
P Player

When you feel you have mastered a series of exercises, go back to the beginning and play the same sequences, but this time vary the speed and spin imparted to the ball. Two examples of ways to do this are:

Exercise 1

Play the push with

1 little backspin
2 more backspin
3 severe backspin

Exercise 15

Play the topspin with

1 little spin (almost a flat hit)
2 more spin
3 severe spin
4 slow pace
5 medium pace
6 fast pace

Where practicable, the player should also vary the exercises by taking the ball 'early – peak – late' so that he also gets used to playing the ball at different timing positions as shown in the diagram below.

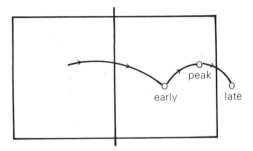

Finally, a word about fitness. No player in any sport can hope to achieve success if the body and mind are not tuned up to maximum fitness, and in table tennis particularly the player must be mentally alert and physically agile.

This book is *not* intended for 'ping-pong' players – it is intended for the player who takes the game seriously and wants to reach his maximum potential in one of the fastest and most exacting indoor sports in the world.

But remember – no amount of practice under set conditions can compensate for actual competitive match play – therefore it is of vital importance to play competitively as soon as possible and thus make capital of the effort you have put into your training.

Exercises : section I

CONSISTENCY, CONTROL AND MOBILITY

The exercises in this section are intended to give the player confidence in making the correct stroke and distributing the ball accurately to all parts of the table from different positions.

1

Controller

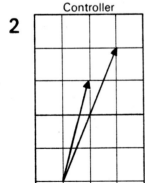

Player

Sequence:
1 *C* B.H. B/S service from position D to target V
2 *P* B.H. push stroke to target V
3 *C* B.H. push stroke to target V

Repeat strokes 2 and 3 to maintain steady B.H. push strokes in continuous sequence.

10	20	30	40	50

2

Controller

Player

Sequence:
1 *C* B.H. B/S service from position D to target V
2 *P* B.H. push stroke to target V
3 *C* B.H. push stroke to target V
4 *P* B.H. push stroke to target Z
5 *C* B.H. push stroke to target V

10	20	30	40	50

Sequence:

1 *C* B.H. B/S service from position D to target D
2 *P* B.H. push stroke to target A
3 *C* F.H. push stroke to target D
4 *P* B.H. push stroke to target B/C
5 *C* B.H. push stroke to target D
6 *P* B.H. push stroke to target D
7 *C* B.H. push stroke to target D

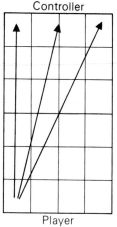

Controller

3

Player

| 10 | 20 | 30 | 40 | 50 |

Sequence:

1 *C* B/S service from position B/C to target C/B
2 *P* B.H. push stroke to target J
3 *C* F.H. push stroke to target C/B
4 *P* B.H. push stroke to target D
5 *C* B.H. push stroke to target C/B

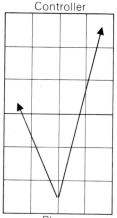

Controller

4

Player

| 10 | 20 | 30 | 40 | 50 |

Sequence:

1 *C* B.H. B/S service from position D to target D
2 *P* B.H. push stroke to target V
3 *C* B.H. push stroke to target C/B
4 *P* B.H. push stroke to target D

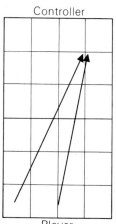

Controller

5

Player

| 10 | 20 | 30 | 40 | 50 |

6

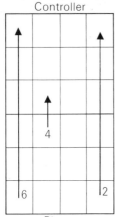

Controller

4

6   2

Player

Sequence:
1 *C* F.H. B/S service from position A to target A
2 *P* B.H. push stroke to target D
3 *C* B.H. push stroke to target Z
4 *P* B.H. push stroke to target Z
5 *C* B.H. push stroke to target D
6 *P* B.H. push stroke to target A
7 *C* F.H. push stroke to target A

This exercise requires both players to move quickly into position before playing the stroke.

10	20	30	40	50

7

Controller

A	B	C	D
H			E
J	K	L	M

V

Player

Controller's task

This exercise begins with the controller playing a backspin service from position C/D to target V. Each following stroke in the rally must be played *accurately* to target V using only a push stroke. This requires the controller to move quickly into the correct position before making a stroke.

Player's task

The player's task is to play the ball to each target area indicated on the diagram, starting with target A and progressing in a clockwise direction, using only a B.H. push stroke.

10	20	30	40	50

8

Controller

Player

Sequence:
1 *C* F.H. B/S service from position A to target X
2 *P* F.H. push stroke to target X
3 *C* Return the ball to target X using a push stroke.

Note It is usually much easier to control accurately using a backhand stroke and I would advise the controller to try this method by taking up a backhand position from area A.

10	20	30	40	50

Sequence:

1 *C* B/S service from position A to target X
2 *P* F.H. push stroke to target Z
3 *C* Return ball to target X using a push stroke
4 *P* F.H. push stroke to target X
5 *C* Return ball to target X using a push stroke

Controller

9

Player

| 10 | 20 | 30 | 40 | 50 |

Sequence:

1 *C* F.H. B/S service from position A to target X
2 *P* F.H. push stroke to target D
3 *C* B.H. push stroke to target X
4 *P* F.H. push stroke to target B/C
5 *C* B.H. push stroke to target X
6 *P* F.H. push stroke to target A
7 *C* F.H. push stroke to target X

Controller

10

Player

| 10 | 20 | 30 | 40 | 50 |

Sequence:

1 *C* B.H. B/S service from position D to target C/B
2 *P* F.H. push stroke to target J
3 *C* F.H. push stroke to target C/B
4 *P* F.H. push stroke to target D
5 *C* B.H. push stroke to target C/B

Controller

11

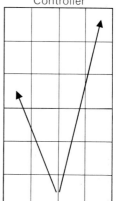

Player

| 10 | 20 | 30 | 40 | 50 |

12

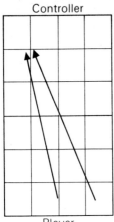

Controller

Player

Sequence:
1. *C* B/S service from position A to target A
2. *P* F.H. push stroke to target X
3. *C* Return ball to target C/B using a push stroke
4. *P* F.H. push stroke to target X
5. *C* Return ball to target A using a push stroke

| 10 | 20 | 30 | 40 | 50 |

13

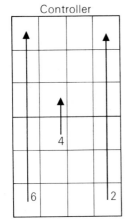

Controller

Player

Sequence:
1. *C* F.H. B/S service from position A to target A
2. *P* F.H. push stroke to target D
3. *C* B.H. push stroke to target Z
4. *P* F.H. push stroke to target Z
5. *C* B.H. push stroke to target D
6. *P* F.H. push stroke to target A
7. *C* F.H. push stroke to target A

| 10 | 20 | 30 | 40 | 50 |

14

Controller

A	B	C	D
H			E
J	K	L	M

—X—

Player

Controller's task

This exercise begins with the controller playing a backspin service from position A to target X. Each following stroke in the rally must be played *accurately* to target X using only a push stroke. This requires the controller to move quickly into the correct position before making a stroke.

Player's task

The player's task is to play the ball to each target area indicated on the diagram, starting with target A and progressing in a clockwise direction, using only a F.H. push stroke.

| 10 | 20 | 30 | 40 | 50 |

Sequence:

1 *C* Serve with very little B/S from position A to target X

2 *P* F.H. T/S drive to target X

3 *C* Return the ball to target X using a half volley block shot

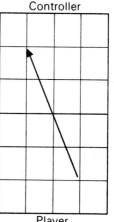

Controller

15

Player

10	20	30	40	50

Sequence:

1 *C* Using a slight amount of B/S, serve from position A to target X

2 *P* F.H. T/S drive to target X

3 *C* Return the ball to target X using a half volley block shot

4 *P* F.H. T/S drive to target Z

5 *C* Half volley block shot to target X

Controller

16

Player

10	20	30	40	50

Sequence:

1 *C* Play a fairly bouncy service from position A to target X

2 *P* F.H. T/S drive to target A

3 *C* Half volley block shot to target X

4 *P* F.H. T/S drive to target Z

5 *C* Half volley block shot to target X

6 *P* F.H. T/S drive to target D

7 *C* Half volley block shot to target X

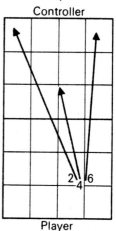

Controller

17

Player

10	20	30	40	50

71

18

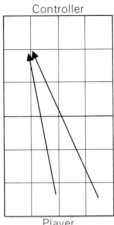

Controller

Player

Sequence:

1 *C* Play a fairly bouncy service from position A to target A

2 *P* F.H. T/S drive to target X

3 *C* Half volley block shot to target C/B

4 *P* F.H. T/S drive to target X

5 *C* Half volley block shot to target A

10	20	30	40	50

19

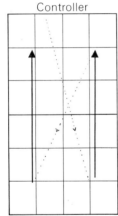

Controller

Player

Sequence:

1 *C* Use a slow bouncy service from position B to target X

2 *P* F.H. T/S drive to target V

3 *C* Half volley block shot to target V

4 *P* F.H. T/S drive to target X

5 *C* Half volley block shot to target X

This exercise requires both players to move very quickly into position before making the stroke. The dotted lines indicate the direction of the controller's ball.

10	20	30	40	50

20

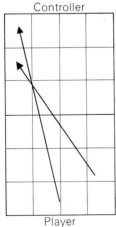

Controller

Player

Sequence:

1 *C* Slow B/S service from position A to target H

2 *P* F.H. T/S drive to target H

3 *C* Half volley block shot to target C/B

4 *P* F.H. T/S drive to target A

5 *C* Half volley block shot to target H

10	20	30	40	50

Sequence:
1 *C* Slow bouncy service from position A to target D
2 *P* F.H. T/S drive to target A
3 *C* Half volley block shot to target D
4 *P* F.H. T/S drive to target D
5 *C* Half volley block shot to target D

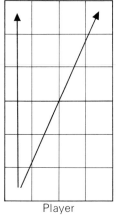

10	20	30	40	50

Controller's task

Using only half volley block returns the controller must play each ball to target X. A slow bouncy service is needed to start the rally.

Player's task

The player must return the ball to each of the targets indicated on the diagram using only F.H. T/S drives and starting with target H. He should then progress to the other targets in a clockwise direction.

10	20	30	40	50

EXERCISES 23 to 30

Repeat exercises 15 to 22 but this time with the controller playing half volley drives. In other words the tempo of the play is increased.

EXERCISES 31 to 38

Repeat exercises 15 to 22 but with the controller now playing backspin defensive returns. The player should refer to the section of the book dealing with this particular aspect of stroke production.

EXERCISES 39 to 46

Repeat exercises 15 to 22 with the controller playing topspin counter hitting returns. The method of counter-driving is explained in the first part of the book (p. 54) and should be studied again as a reminder to make the correct movements.

47

Controller

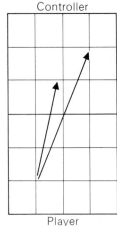

Player

Sequence:
1 *C* Slow bouncy service from position D to target V
2 *P* B.H. T/S drive to target V
3 *C* B.H. half volley block shot to target V

| 10 | 20 | 30 | 40 | 50 |

48

Controller

Player

Sequence:
1 *C* Slow bouncy service from position D to target V
2 *P* B.H. T/S drive to target V
3 *C* Half volley block shot to target V
4 *P* B.H. T/S drive to target Z
5 *C* Half volley block shot to target V

| 10 | 20 | 30 | 40 | 50 |

49

Controller

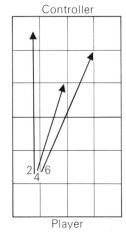

Player

Sequence:
1 *C* Slow bouncy service from position D to target V
2 *P* B.H. T/S drive to target A
3 *C* Half volley block shot to target V
4 *P* B.H. T/S drive to target Z
5 *C* Half volley block shot to target V
6 *P* B.H. T/S drive to target V
7 *C* Half volley block shot to target V

| 10 | 20 | 30 | 40 | 50 |

Sequence:

1 *C* Slow bouncy service from position D to target D
2 *P* B.H. T/S drive to target V
3 *C* Half volley block shot to target C/B
4 *P* B.H. T/S drive to target V
5 *C* Half volley block shot to target D

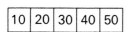

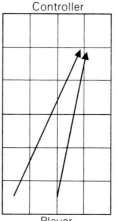

Controller

50

Player

Sequence:

1 *C* Slow B/S service from position D to target D
2 *P* B.H. T/S drive to target A
3 *C* Half volley block shot to target C/B
4 *P* B.H. T/S drive to target D
5 *C* Half volley block to target D

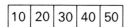

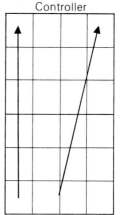

Controller

51

Player

Sequence:

1 *C* Slow B/S service from position D to target E
2 *P* B.H. T/S drive to target E
3 *C* Half volley block shot to target C/B
4 *P* B.H. T/S drive to target D
5 *C* Half volley block shot to target E

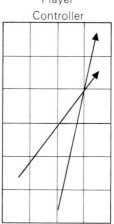

Controller

52

Player

53

Controller

A	B	C	D
F			E
	V		

Player

Controller's task

Start the rally with a slow B/S service from position D to target V. Make each return to target V using only a half volley block shot.

Player's task

Using only B.H. T/S drives, play the ball to each of the targets indicated on the diagram, starting with target F and progressing in a clockwise direction.

EXERCISES 54 to 60

Repeat exercises 47 to 53 but with the controller playing half volley drives, thus speeding up the exercises.

EXERCISES 61 to 67

Repeat exercises 47 to 53 with the controller playing backspin defensive returns.

EXERCISES 68 to 74

Repeat exercises 47 to 53 with the controller playing topspin counter hitting returns.

75

Controller

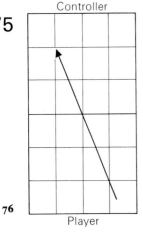

Player

Sequence:

1 *C* Fast T/S service from position B to target A
2 *P* F.H. B/S stroke to target X
3 *C* F.H. T/S drive to target A

Sequence:

1 *C* Serve F.H. fast T/S from position C to target C/B
2 *P* F.H. B/S stroke to target J
3 *C* F.H. T/S drive to target C/B
4 *P* F.H. B/S stroke to target B/C
5 *C* F.H. T/S drive to target C/B

Controller

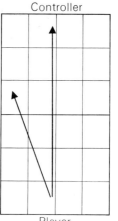

76

Player

Sequence:

1 *C* F.H. T/S service from position B to target X
2 *P* F.H. B/S stroke to target A
3 *C* F.H. T/S drive to target X
4 *P* F.H. B/S stroke to target Z
5 *C* B.H. T/S drive to target X
6 *P* F.H. B/S stroke to target D
7 *C* B.H. T/S drive to target X

Controller

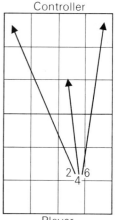

77

Player

Sequence:

1 *C* Fast F.H. T/S service from position B to target A
2 *P* F.H. B/S stroke to target A
3 *C* F.H. T/S drive to target C/B
4 *P* F.H. B/S stroke to target A
5 *C* F.H. T/S drive to target A

Controller

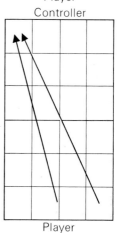

78

Player

79

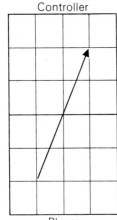

Controller

A	B	C	D
J	K	L	M
	C	B	

Player

Controller's task
Start the rally with a fast T/S service to target C/B.
Return each ball to target C/B using either F.H.
or B.H. T/S drives as appropriate.

Player's task
Play alternately long and short F.H. B/S strokes to
the targets indicated on the diagram in the following order:
A – K – C – M – D – L – B – J

10	20	30	40	50

80

Controller

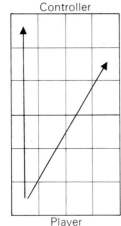

Player

Sequence:
1 *C* Fast B.H. T/S service from position D to target V
2 *P* B.H. B/S stroke to target V
3 *C* B.H. T/S drive to target V

10	20	30	40	50

81

Controller

Sequence:
1 *C* Fast F.H. T/S service from position A to
   target D
2 *P* B.H. B/S stroke to target E
3 *C* B.H. T/S drive to target D
4 *P* B.H. B/S stroke to target A
5 *C* F.H. T/S drive to target D

10	20	30	40	50

Player

Sequence:

1 *C* Fast F.H. T/S service from position A to target D
2 *P* B.H. B/S stroke to target A
3 *C* F.H. T/S drive to target D
4 *P* B.H. B/S stroke to target Z
5 *C* B.H. T/S drive to target D
6 *P* B.H. B/S stroke to target D
7 *C* B.H. T/S drive to target D

10	20	30	40	50

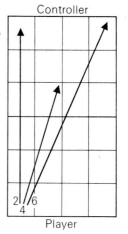

82

Controller / Player

2 / 6
4

Sequence:

1 *C* Fast F.H. T/S service from position C to target D
2 *P* B.H. B/S stroke to target A
3 *C* F.H. T/S drive to target C/B
4 *P* B.H. B/S stroke to target B/C
5 *C* F.H. T/S drive to target D

10	20	30	40	50

83

Controller / Player

Controller's task

Start the rally with a fast T/S service to target C/B.
Return each ball to target C/B using either F.H. or
B.H. T/S drives as appropriate.

Player's task

Play alternate long and short B.H. B/S strokes to the
targets indicated on the diagram in the following
order: A – K – C – M – D – L – B – J

10	20	30	40	50

84

Controller

A	B	C	D
J	K	L	M
		C	B

Player

85

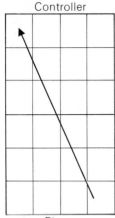

Controller

Player

Sequence:

1 *C* Long B/S service from position B to target A
2 *P* F.H. looped T/S drive to target A
3 *C* F.H. 'heavy' B/S stroke to target A

| 10 | 20 | 30 | 40 | 50 |

86

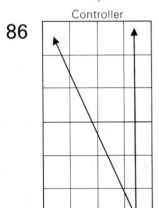

Controller

Player

Sequence:

1 *C* Heavy B/S service from position A to target A
2 *P* F.H. looped T/S drive to target D
3 *C* B.H. 'heavy' B/S stroke to target A
4 *P* F.H. looped T/S drive to target A
5 *C* F.H. 'heavy' B/S stroke to target A

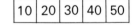

| 10 | 20 | 30 | 40 | 50 |

87

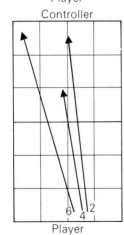

Controller

Player

Sequence:

1 *C* Fast B/S service from position B to target B
2 *P* Fast F.H. looped T/S drive to target B/C
3 *C* F.H. B/S stroke to target B
4 *P* Slow F.H. looped T/S drive to target Z
5 *C* F.H. B/S stroke to target B
6 *P* Fast F.H. looped T/S drive to target A
7 *C* F.H. B/S stroke to target B

| 10 | 20 | 30 | 40 | 50 |

Sequence:

1 *C* Heavy B/S service from position B/C to target A
2 *P* F.H. looped T/S drive to target B/C
3 *C* Heavy B/S stroke to target C
4 *P* F.H. looped T/S drive to target B/C
5 *C* Heavy B/S stroke to target A

This exercise requires the player to move very quickly into position before making the stroke.

10	20	30	40	50

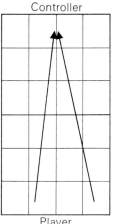

88

Sequence:

1 *C* Heavy B/S service from position A to target A
2 *P* Slow F.H. looped T/S drive to target D
3 *C* B.H. B/S stroke to target A
4 *P* Fast F.H. looped T/S drive to target H
5 *C* F.H. B/S return to target A

10	20	30	40	50

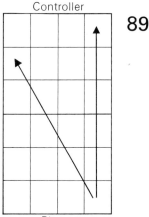

89

Sequence:

1 *C* B/S service played diagonally from position A to target H
2 *P* F.H. T/S looped drive with S/S to target H
3 *C* F.H. B/S stroke to target H

10	20	30	40	50

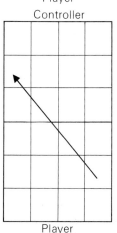

90

91

Controller

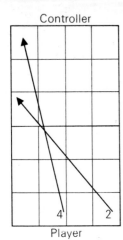

Player

Sequence:

1 *C* Heavy b/s service from position A to target A
2 *P* Slow F.H. looped t/s drive with s/s to target J
3 *C* F.H. b/s stroke to target C/B
4 *P* Fast F.H. looped t/s drive with s/s to target A
5 *C* F.H. b/s stroke to target A

10	20	30	40	50

EXERCISES 92 to 99

Repeat exercises 85 to 91 with the controller this time playing half volley block returns.

EXERCISES 100 to 106

Repeat exercises 85 to 91 with the controller playing counter looped returns.

These exercises are very difficult to perform accurately and should be attempted by experienced players only.

COMBINATION OF STROKES

The exercises contained in this section have been selected to give the player experience in combining the various strokes already practised. When moving to different positions, move quickly but lightly, maintaining a good balance at all times.

Sequence:

1 *C* B/S service from position B/C to target X
2 *P* F.H. push stroke to target B/C
3 *C* B.H. push stroke to target V
4 *P* B.H. push stroke to target B/C
5 *C* B.H. push stroke to target X

Controller

107

Player

10	20	30	40	50

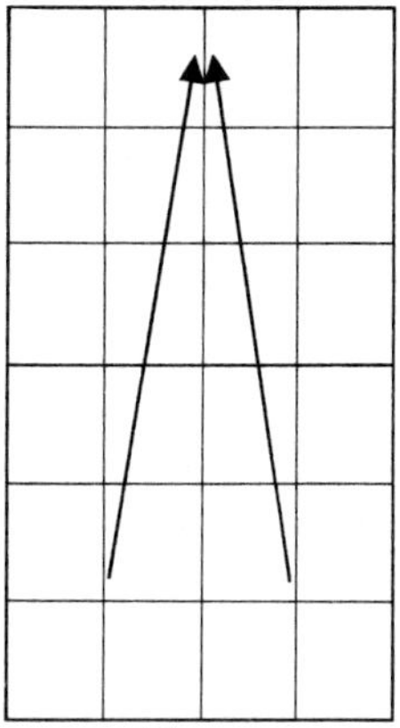

Sequence:

1 *C* Long B/S service from position B/C to target A
2 *P* Late F.H. push stroke to target B/C
3 *C* B.H. push stroke to target L
4 *P* Early B.H. push stroke to target B/C
5 *C* B.H. push stroke to target A

Controller

108

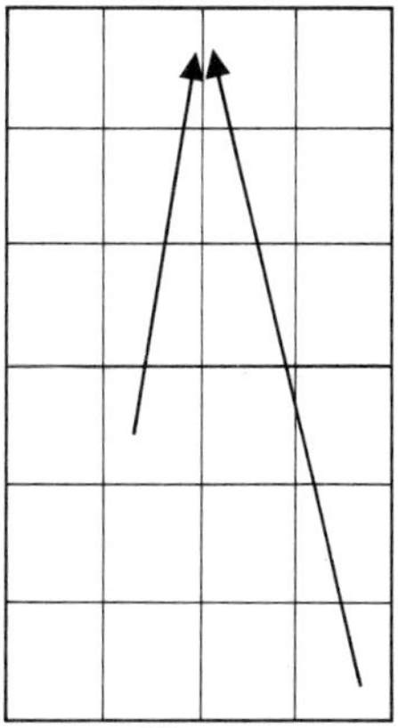

Player

10	20	30	40	50

109

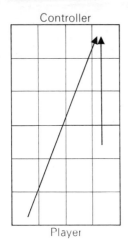

Controller

Player

Sequence:

1 *C* Long B/S service from position D to target D
2 *P* Late B.H. push stroke to target D
3 *C* B.H. push stroke to target J
4 *P* Early F.H. push stroke to target D
5 *C* B.H. push stroke to target D

10	20	30	40	50

110

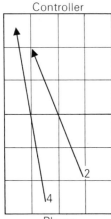

Controller

Player

Sequence:

1 *C* F.H. B/S service from position A to target X
2 *P* F.H. push stroke to target X
3 *C* F.H. push stroke to target B
4 *P* F.H. T/S drive to target A
5 *C* F.H. B/S stroke to target X

10	20	30	40	50

111

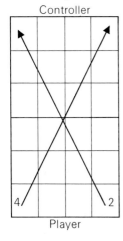

Controller

Player

Sequence:

1 *C* B.H. B/S service from position D to target A
2 *P* F.H. T/S drive to target A
3 *C* F.H. B/S stroke to target D
4 *P* B.H. T/S drive to target D
5 *C* B.H. B/S stroke to target A

10	20	30	40	50

Sequence:

1 *C* Fast F.H. T/S service from position B to target X
2 *P* F.H. half volley block shot to target X
3 *C* F.H. T/S drive to target C
4 *P* B.H. half volley block shot to target X
5 *C* F.H. T/S drive to target X

10	20	30	40	50

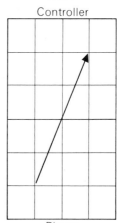

Controller

112

Player

Sequence:

1 *C* Fast B.H. T/S service from position D to target V
2 *P* B.H. half volley block shot to target V
3 *C* B.H. push stroke to target V
4 *P* B.H. T/S drive to target V
5 *C* B.H. B/S stroke to target V
6 *P* B.H. push stroke to target V
7 *C* B.H. T/S drive to target V

10	20	30	40	50

Controller

113

Player

Sequence:

1 *C* Fast F.H. T/S service from position A to target X
2 *P* F.H. half volley block shot to target X
3 *C* F.H. push stroke to target X
4 *P* F.H. T/S drive to target X
5 *C* F.H. B/S stroke to target X
6 *P* F.H. push stroke to target X
7 *C* F.H. T/S drive to target X

10	20	30	40	50

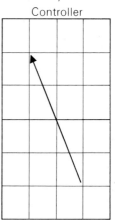

Controller

114

Player

115

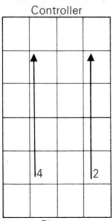

Controller

Player

Sequence:
1. *C* Slow F.H. T/S service from position B to target X
2. *P* F.H. T/S drive to target V
3. *C* B.H. half volley block shot to target V
4. *P* B.H. T/S drive to target X
5. *C* F.H. half volley block to target X

| 10 | 20 | 30 | 40 | 50 |

116

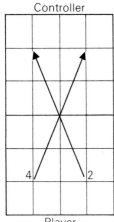

Controller

Player

Sequence:
1. *C* Slow B.H. T/S service from position C/D to target X
2. *P* F.H. T/S drive to target X
3. *C* F.H. half volley block shot to target V
4. *P* B.H. T/S drive to target V
5. *C* B.H. half volley block shot to target X

| 10 | 20 | 30 | 40 | 50 |

117

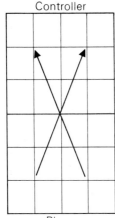

Controller

Player

Sequence:
1. *C* Fast T/S service from position C/D to target X
2. *P* F.H. counter drive to target X
3. *C* F.H. counter drive to target V
4. *P* B.H. counter drive to target V
5. *C* B.H. counter drive to target X

| 10 | 20 | 30 | 40 | 50 |

86

Sequence:
1 *C* Fast F.H. T/S service from position A to target X
2 *P* F.H. counter drive to target V
3 *C* B.H. counter drive to target V
4 *P* B.H. B/S stroke to target X
5 *C* F.H. T/S drive to target X

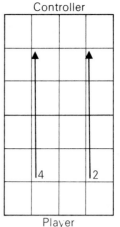

118

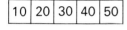

Sequence:
1 *C* Fast F.H. T/S service from position A to target A
2 *P* F.H. T/S drive to target A
3 *C* F.H. T/S drive to target A
4 *P* B.H. T/S drive to target A
5 *C* F.H. T/S drive to target A

The player is required to move very quickly from the F.H. 'ready' position to the B.H. 'ready' position.

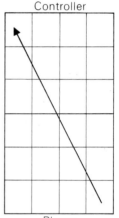

119

Sequence:
1 *C* Fast F.H. T/S service from position A to target A
2 *P* B.H. half volley block shot to target A
3 *C* F.H. T/S drive to target A
4 *P* F.H. counter drive to target A
5 *C* F.H. counter drive to target A

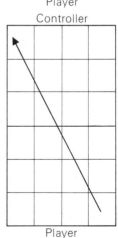

120

| 10 | 20 | 30 | 40 | 50 |

121

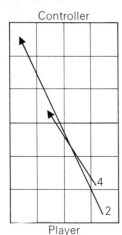

Controller

Player

Sequence:

1 *C* Heavy F.H. B/S service from position A to target A
2 *P* F.H. looped T/S drive to target A
3 *C* F.H. B/S stroke to target X
4 *P* F.H. drop shot to target K
5 *C* F.H. push stroke to target A

| 10 | 20 | 30 | 40 | 50 |

122

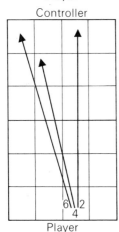

Controller

Player

Sequence:

1 *C* F.H. B/S service from position A to target B
2 *P* Fast F.H. looped T/S drive to target C
3 *C* B.H. half volley block shot to target B
4 *P* Fast F.H. drive to target A
5 *C* F.H. half volley block shot to target B
6 *P* Slow F.H. looped T/S drive to target X
7 *C* F.H. half volley block shot to target B

| 10 | 20 | 30 | 40 | 50 |

123

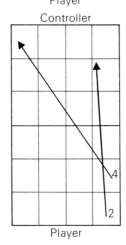

Controller

Player

Sequence:

1 *C* F.H. B/S service from position A to target A
2 *P* Slow F.H. looped T/S drive to target V
3 *C* B.H. B/S stroke to target H
4 *P* F.H. looped T/S drive with S/S to target A
5 *C* F.H. B/S stroke to target A

| 10 | 20 | 30 | 40 | 50 |

Sequence:

1 *C* F.H. B/S service from position A to target H
2 *P* F.H. looped T/S drive with S/S to target H
3 *C* F.H. B/S stroke to target H
4 *P* F.H. drop shot to target M
5 *C* B.H. push stroke to target H

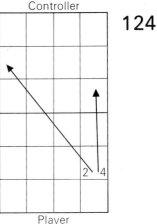

124

10	20	30	40	50

Sequence:

1 *C* Fast F.H. T/S service from position A to target A
2 *P* F.H. B/S stroke to target A
3 *C* F.H. T/S drive to target B
4 *P* B.H. counter drive to target D
5 *C* B.H. counter drive to target E
6 *P* B.H. counter drive to target E
7 *C* B.H. counter drive to target A

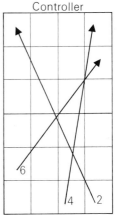

125

10	20	30	40	50

Sequence:

1 *C* Fast F. H. T/S service from position A to target A
2 *P* F.H. B/S stroke to target X
3 *C* F.H. push stroke to target Z
4 *P* F.H. push stroke to target X
5 *C* F.H. T/S drive to target A

126

10	20	30	40	50

127

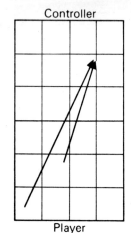

Controller

Player

Sequence:

1 *C* Fast B.H. T/S service from position D to target D
2 *P* B.H. B/S stroke to target V
3 *C* B.H. push stroke to target Z
4 *P* B.H. push stroke to target V
5 *C* B.H. T/S drive to target D

128

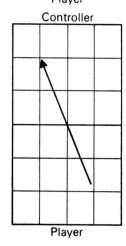

Controller

Player

Sequence:

1 *C* F.H. B/S service from position A to target X
2 *P* F.H. T/S drive to target X
3 *C* F.H. B/S stroke to target X
4 *P* F.H. push stroke to target X
5 *C* F.H. push stroke to target X

PROGRESSIVE TRAINING

The exercises in this section are designed to give the player a progressive build up to match-play situations.

The first few exercises can be practised by all players but have purposely been made fairly easy, so that the inexperienced players will be quite capable of performing the tasks described.

The programme gets progressively harder towards the end of the section.

Exercises : section 3

Sequence:

1 *C* Fast F.H. B/S service from position A to target A
2 *P* F.H. late push stroke to target A
3 *C* F.H. short push stroke to target K
4 *P* F.H. early push stroke to target K
5 *C* F.H. push stroke to target A

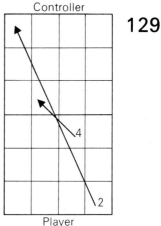

129

Sequence:

1 *C* F.H. B/S service from position A to target A
2 *P* F.H. late push stroke to target A
3 *C* F.H. push stroke to target E
4 *P* B.H. early push stroke to target A
5 *C* F.H. push stroke to target A

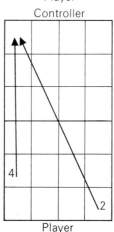

130

Note You may notice that several of the exercises have been described earlier in the book, but these have been selected again to show the progressive nature of this particular type of training.

131

Controller

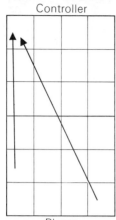

Player

Controller's task
As in the last exercise the controller begins the rally with a F.H. B/S service, but this time he plays at random to targets A and E using only a push stroke.

Player's task
Since the player cannot tell beforehand to which target the oncoming ball will be directed, he must be very alert and ready to move quickly into position. He must return every ball to target A using either a late F.H. push stroke (from position A) or an early B.H. push stroke (from position D).

10	20	30	40	50

132

Controller

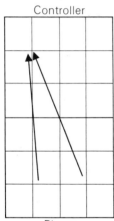

Player

Sequence:
1 *C* F.H. T/S service from position A to target X
2 *P* F.H. counter drive to target X
3 *C* F.H. counter drive to target V
4 *P* F.H. counter drive to target X
5 *C* F.H. counter drive to target X

10	20	30	40	50

133

Controller

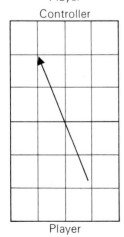

Player

Sequence:
1 *C* F.H. T/S service from position A to target X
2 *P* F.H. counter drive to target X
3 *C* F.H. T/S drive to target X
4 *P* F.H. B/S stroke to target X
5 *C* F.H. T/S drive to target X

10	20	30	40	50

EXERCISES 134 and 135

Repeat exercises 132 and 133 but the controller now has the choice of using either a flat hit or T/S drive.

Players must return all topspin balls using chop, and must counter drive all flat hit returns.

EXERCISES 136 to 139

Repeat exercises 132 to 135 with players using backhand returns. The appropriate opposite targets should be used.

Sequence:

1 *C* F.H. T/S service from position A to target X
2 *P* F.H. counter drive to target X
3 *C* F.H. counter drive to target V
4 *P* B.H. counter drive to target X
5 *C* F.H. counter drive to target X

Controller

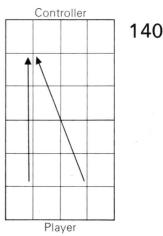

140

Player

10	20	30	40	50

Controller

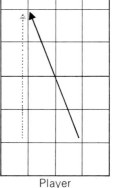

141

Controller's task

Start the rally with a F.H. T/S service from position A to target X. Maintain steady F.H. counter drives to target X but occasionally at random hit a ball to target V.

Player's task

Play F.H. counter drives to target X but be ready to play a B.H. counter drive to target X against the ball played suddenly to target V.

10	20	30	40	50

Player

142

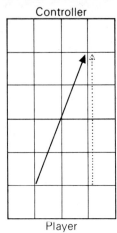

Controller

Player

This exercise is similar to No. 141, but this time the continuous play is from V to V using B.H. counter drives, with the 'random' ball being played by the controller to target X.

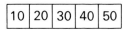

10	20	30	40	50

143

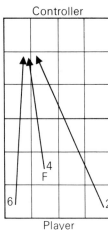

Controller

Player

Sequence:

1 *C* Fast F.H. T/s service from position A to target A
2 *P* F.H. B/s stroke to target A
3 *C* F.H. T/s drive to target F
4 *P* B.H. half volley block shot to target A
5 *C* F.H. push stroke to target D
6 *P* B.H. T/s drive to target X
7 *C* F.H. T/s drive to target A

10	20	30	40	50

EXERCISE 144

Repeat exercise 143 using targets as designated both for the player and the controller in the same sequences, but this time the controller can choose the type of stroke he plays, e.g. instead of playing T/s to F he may decide to chop. This means the player must decide instantly which stroke to play in order to counter the controller's return.

EXERCISE 145

Exercise 143 is again repeated using the same strokes and targets as indicated, but the controller chooses at random the order of his returns. This means that the player must be very alert in order to move quickly into one of the three positions designated.

Taking this same exercise a stage further, the controller can now choose at random: **1** the type of ball he returns i.e. backspin, half volley blocks, or push; and **2** the target to which he plays.

Many clubs and schools throughout the country play table tennis, but unfortunately one finds all too often that the facilities afforded by such establishments leave a lot to be desired.

One of the main problems is that several players have to practice at the same time, and although these training conditions are far from ideal there are certain exercises which can be conducted on one table using three or four players.

I personally feel that using any more than four players to one table achieves very little progress, although I have myself at times been forced by circumstances to have as many as eight players on one table.

Before attempting the exercises in this section, it would be advisable to study the following notes.

1 Always try to arrange your group in such a way that each member is afforded maximum space in which to play.
2 Try to segregate the left-handed players in pairs – this facilitates table organization.
3 If you have a left-handed player with three right-handed players, reverse the stroke play procedure as follows:

Exercises :
section 4

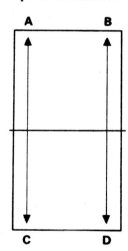

Exercise for four *right-handed* players
A B.H. push to C
C F.H. push to A
B F.H. push to D
D B.H. push to B

However, if player A is *left-handed* then he would play F.H. push to C, thus avoiding a possible collision with player B.

The diagrams below are intended to clarify the location of channels which are described in the text of the exercises that follow. They are indicated in the diagrams by the arrow-headed black lines.

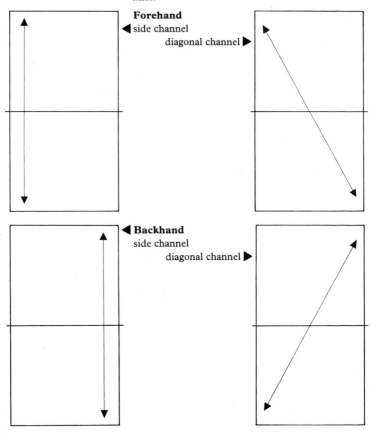

Forehand
◀ side channel
diagonal channel ▶

◀ **Backhand**
side channel
diagonal channel ▶

Players should change positions regularly, moving in a clockwise direction. Remember to go through each exercise several times, changing one aspect of the routine each time. For instance, the same practice can be varied by playing short, medium and long balls and, when practicable, the timing positions may be revised also.

Rather than use letters of the alphabet to indicate the players, which may lead to confusion with the target areas, I have given names to the four players involved.

Order of play
Forehand side channel:

1 *Shaun plays* B.H. B/S service to target D
2 *Craig plays* F.H. push stroke to target A
3 *Shaun plays* B.H. push stroke to target D

Backhand side channel:

1 *Wayne plays* F.H. B/S service to target A
2 *Ivan plays* B.H. push stroke to target D
3 *Wayne plays* F.H. push stroke to target A

10	20	30	40	50

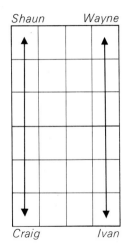

146

Order of play
Forehand diagonal channel:

1 *Shaun plays* B.H. T/S service to target A
2 *Ivan plays* B.H. half volley block shot to target A
3 *Shaun plays* B.H. T/S drive to target A

Backhand diagonal channel:

1 *Craig plays* F.H. T/S service to target D
2 *Wayne plays* F.H. half volley block shot to target D
3 *Craig plays* F.H. T/S drive to target D

10	20	30	40	50

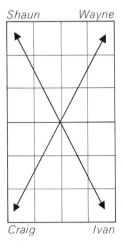

147

148

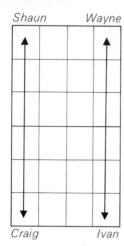

Shaun   Wayne

Craig   Ivan

Order of play

Forehand side channel:

1 *Shaun plays* B.H. B/S service to target D
2 *Craig plays* F.H. T/S drive to target A
3 *Shaun plays* B.H. B/S stroke to target D

Backhand side channel:

1 *Wayne plays* F.H. T/S service to target A
2 *Ivan plays* B.H. B/S stroke to target D
3 *Wayne plays* F.H. T/S drive to target A

| 10 | 20 | 30 | 40 | 50 |

149

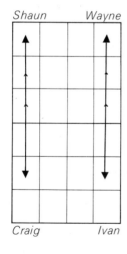

Shaun   Wayne

Craig   Ivan

Order of play

Forehand side channel:

1 *Shaun plays* B.H. B/S service to target E
2 *Craig plays* F.H. push stroke to target J
3 *Shaun plays* B.H. push stroke to target E
4 *Craig plays* F.H. push stroke to target H
5 *Shaun plays* B.H. push stroke to target E
6 *Craig plays* F.H. push stroke to target A
7 *Shaun plays* B.H. push stroke to target E

Backhand side channel:

1 *Wayne plays* F.H. B/S service to target H
2 *Ivan plays* B.H. push stroke to target M
3 *Wayne plays* F.H. push stroke to target H
4 *Ivan plays* B.H. push stroke to target E
5 *Wayne plays* F.H. push stroke to target H
6 *Ivan plays* B.H. push stroke to target D
7 *Wayne plays* F.H. push stroke to target H

| 10 | 20 | 30 | 40 | 50 |

Order of play
Forehand diagonal channel:

1 *Shaun serves* fast B.H. T/S service to target A
2 *Ivan plays* B.H. B/S stroke to target A
3 *Shaun plays* B.H. push stroke to target A
4 *Ivan plays* B.H. push stroke to target A
5 *Shaun plays* B.H. T/S drive to target A

Backhand diagonal channel:

1 *Wayne serves* fast F.H. T/S service to target D
2 *Craig plays* F.H. B/S stroke to target D
3 *Wayne plays* F.H. push stroke to target D
4 *Craig plays* F.H. push stroke to target D
5 *Wayne plays* F.H. T/S drive to target D

10	20	30	40	50

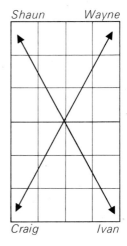

150

Shaun   *Wayne*

Craig   *Ivan*

Order of play
Forehand side channel:

Shaun starts the rally with a B.H. T/S service to target D, and thereafter plays B.H. counter drives to the same target, but occasionally (at random) he plays a B.H. B/S stroke.

Craig plays every ball using a F.H. counter drive to target A, except when his partner makes a 'chopped' defensive return, in which case he plays a F.H. T/S drive.

Backhand side channel:

Wayne serves using F.H. T/S to target A and then counter drives each ball with his forehand but, like *Shaun*, he too can choose to slip in a F.H. 'chop' at any time in the rally.

Ivan has to return each ball with B.H. counter drives to target D, and must be ready to play a B.H. T/S drive to any ball which has been 'chopped'.

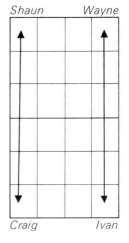

151

Shaun   *Wayne*

Craig   *Ivan*

10	20	30	40	50

152

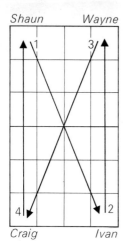

Shaun   Wayne

Craig   Ivan

Sequence:

1 *Shaun plays* F.H. T/S service to target A
2 *Ivan plays* B.H. B/S stroke to target D
3 *Wayne plays* B.H. T/S drive to target D
4 *Craig plays* F.H. counter drive to target A
5 *Shaun plays* F.H. T/S drive to target A

N.B. After playing his shot, the player should move out to allow his partner more freedom of space.

10	20	30	40	50

To make progress, while practising the following exercises, it is necessary for each player in turn to stand down. By rotating in a clockwise direction, each player has the opportunity to practise the different strokes from each of the three positions on the table.

If you change positions every five minutes, you will then have fifteen minutes' continuous practice and a five-minute rest. Alternatively, the exercises can be turned into a game, whereby the *single* player wins a point if either of the controllers makes an error. If the player makes an error (e.g. he plays into the net or over the end of the table or misses the target area, etc.) he then has to stand down, while the other three players in the group move round one position on the table. Each time you are at the player's end, add up your previous scores until one player accumulates 21 points and thus becomes the winner.

> N.B. The black lines on the diagrams indicate the player's ball and the dotted lines indicate the controller's ball.

Sequence:

1 *Controller Q* F.H. B/S service from position D to target X
2 *Player* F.H. T/S drive to target X
3 *Controller P* B.H. half volley block shot to target V
4 *Player* F.H. T/S drive to target V
5 *Controller Q* F.H. B/S stroke to target X

> N.B. Stage 4 of this rally requires the player to move extremely quickly into position before playing the shot.

10	20	30	40	50

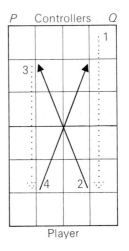

153

154

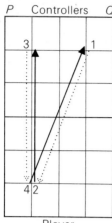

Sequence:

1 *Controller Q* B.H. T/S service to target V
2 *Player* B.H. counter drive to target X
3 *Controller P* F.H. counter drive to target V
4 *Player* B.H. counter drive to target V
5 *Controller Q* B.H. counter drive to target V

10	20	30	40	50

155

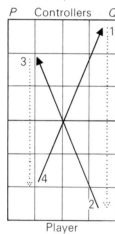

Sequence:

1 *Controller Q* Fast B.H. T/S service to target A
2 *Player* F.H. B/S stroke to target X
3 *Controller P* B.H. push stroke to target V
4 *Player* B.H. T/S drive to target D
5 *Controller Q* B.H. counter drive to target A

10	20	30	40	50

156

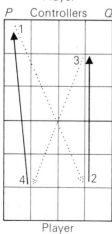

Sequence:

1 *Controller P* F.H. B/S service to target X
2 *Player* F.H. looped T/S drive to target V
3 *Controller Q* B.H. half volley block shot to target V
4 *Player* B.H. flat hit to target A
5 *Controller P* F.H. B/S stroke to target X

10	20	30	40	50

Sequence:

1 *Controller P* F.H. T/S service to target A
2 *Player* F.H. counter drive to target V
3 *Controller Q* B.H. counter drive to target V
4 *Player* B.H. counter drive to target A
5 *Controller P* F.H. counter drive to target A

10	20	30	40	50

157

EXERCISE 158

Repeat exercise 154 but this time the controllers
may play the occasional ball at random to target X,
which will necessitate the player moving quickly
to return the 'loose' ball while still having to
maintain the correct sequence of the rally.

Sequence:

1 *Controller P* F.H. T/S service to target A
2 *Player* F.H. B/S stroke to target D
3 *Controller Q* F.H. looped T/S drive to target E
4 *Player* B.H. half volley block shot to target A
5 *Controller P* F.H. flat hit to target A

10	20	30	40	50

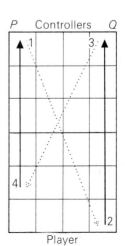

159

160

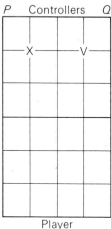

P Controllers Q

X   V

Player

For this exercise the controllers may play to any part of the table, at random, using any stroke of their choice.

The player may return the ball with any stroke of his choice but he must alternate the direction of his returns between target X and target V.

| 10 | 20 | 30 | 40 | 50 |

National proficiency awards

Now that you have worked through the exercises you should be capable of playing table tennis reasonably well. To help you to assess your standard of play, I would suggest that you test your skills by taking the National Proficiency Awards, which are printed in full on the following pages. The tests in each section have been carefully arranged by a panel of experts to test the all-round skills of the table tennis player. However, from time to time, the National Coaching Committee may decide to vary some of the tests, and you should therefore write to the National Awards Organizer before taking the tests, to get any updated alterations. All enquiries should be addressed to:

The National Awards Organizer
71 Maplin Way
Thorpe Bay
Essex

Please enclose a stamped addressed envelope.

HALEX PROFICIENCY AWARD – BRONZE STANDARD

1 *All backhand push control :* (from 2 points, returned to 1 target)
Using sound footwork for training, return 40 slow push shots (which have been placed, slowly, by the Controller from B, alternately to area C and area D). Candidate to use only backhand push strokes, all played back to area B. (See diagram on page 111 for areas.) Required: 40 successes before 6th error.

2 *All forehand slow topspin roll :*
Against gentle returns from the controller, play 40 roll strokes, maintaining direction on one diagonal only, without increasing speed. Required: As test 1.

3 *Combined control :*
Return 40 slow balls from the controller by playing, in strict alternation, backhand push and forehand roll, while maintaining direction on one diagonal only. Required: As test 1.

4 *Backhand block returns :*
Against medium topspin from the controller, return the ball by simple rebound technique, i.e. straight line 'reflection', from the peak-of-bounce position. Maintain direction on one diagonal. Required: As test 1.

5 *Short touch services :*
a From correct position behind the baseline, serve short forehand service so as to bounce twice in opponent's court.
b As **a** but service with backhand.
Required: 4 successes to be achieved within 8 attempts.

6 *Long topspin services :*
a From correct position, serve with forehand; the ball has to land within 18 in (*c.* 45 cm) of distant baseline.
b As **a** but service with backhand.
Required: 5 successes within 8 attempts.

Notes: i For 'Penholder' styles, for backhand read 'to left of body'.
ii For left-handers, reverse targets (A for B etc.).
iii Two players may be tested simultaneously on one table by using opposite diagonal channel on all above tests except 1.

HALEX PROFICIENCY AWARD –
SILVER STANDARD

Preliminary :

Candidates must have passed the Bronze tests.
Before scoring each test, the Assessor shall require:
a A 'dry land' demonstration of the ensuing stroke
actions.
b That the quality of the practical stroke work is
satisfactory.

1 *Return of service by half volley :*
a Using backhand half volley touch, return
safely 10 services, varied as to topspin and chop
and sidespin.
b As **a** but using forehand half volley touch.
Required: 20 successes (10 + 10) before 6th error.

2 *Combining drive and push, forehand :*
Return 40 balls which have been alternately
pushed and chopped, by using (respectively)
topspin drives and push shots, played alternately,
forehand, on one diagonal.
Required: 40 correct before 6th error.

3 *Combining drive and push, backhand :*
As **2** but using backhand throughout.
Required: As test **2**.

4 *Combining (chopped) defensive returns with
push – forehand :*
Return 40 balls which have been alternately
driven and pushed, on same line, by using,
respectively, backspin defensive returns and
pushes, played alternately on same line – all
forehand. Required: As test **2**.

5 *Combining (chopped) defensive returns with push
– backhand :* As **4** but using backhand throughout.
Required: As test **2**.

6 *Laws, rules, etc. :*
Answer 10 'everyday' questions on laws and
match procedure. Points allowed: complete
answer: 3; correct 'sense': 2; part answer: 1.
Pass score: 22 out of 30.

7 *Maintaining attack against topspin from controller :*
a Maintain 10 triple sequences thus: 2 forehand
drives plus 1 backhand block. Required: 10 good
sequences before 5th error.
b As **a** but sequences of: 2 backhand drives
plus 1 forehand block. Required: As test **7a**.

8 *Service variations :*
Deliver 10 services of varying length, incorporating sidespin, alternately left and right.
3rd error fails.

HALEX PROFICIENCY AWARD –
GOLD STANDARD

Preliminary :
Candidates must have passed the Silver tests.
Candidates must have the approval of an E.T.T.A.
Staff Coach or E.T.T.A. Approved Instructor as
to general level of playing ability and presentation.

1 *Topspin driving under pressure – forehand :*
Play 50 forehand topspin drives, to one point,
against half volley returns which have been
placed alternately to areas C and D. Good
forehand position and footwork required
throughout.
Required: 50 correct before 5th error.

2 *Topspin driving under pressure – backhand :*
As 1 but using backhand topspin drives.
Required: As test 1.

3 *Counter driving, close and distant – forehand :*
Return 20 counter drives by means of forehand
counter drives in sequences of 2 thus: 2 'close',
2 'distant', 2 'close', etc. All returns kept on
same line. 3rd error fails.

4 *Counter driving close and distant – backhand :*
As 3 but using backhand counter drives.
3rd error fails.

5 *Combining forehand and backhand topspin drives :*
Against slow chopped returns, which have been
placed alternately to areas J and K, by playing
20 forehand and backhand topspin drives,
alternately, directed diagonally to areas F and
G. 3rd error fails.

6 *Combining forehand and backhand defensive
returns backspin :*
Return 20 drives, received alternately on
corner areas J and K, by means of,
respectively, forehand and backhand chopped
returns, to area L. 3rd error fails.

7 *Sequences of topspin and backspin strokes :*
Play 15 double sequences of forehand chop
and backhand drive against balls which have
been driven to the forehand and pushed to
the backhand. 4th error fails.

8 *Sequences of topspin and backspin strokes :*
Play the reverse of 7, i.e. 'backhand' for 'forehand' (and vice versa). 4th error fails.

9 *Backhand attack distribution :*
Play 10 triple sequences thus: dropshot to
area E; backhand drive to area F; backhand

drive to area G; and repeat. The controller
returns all balls to area H, from long distance,
with backspin. 4th error fails.
10 *Loop topspin forehand :*
Candidate to demonstrate loop drive 5 times
against chopped returns of suitable length and
strength, to suit his requirements. The aim is
to show understanding of the loop technique,
and a continuity of loop drives is not demanded.

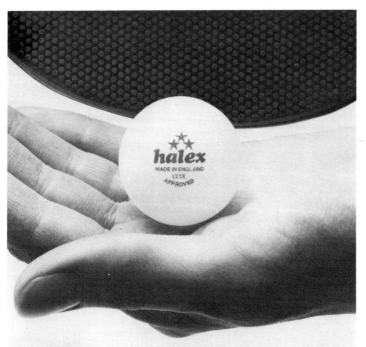

NOTES REGARDING ASSESSMENT

1 Candidates should be allowed to warm up.
2 If only one item is failed, a second attempt at that item may be made the same day. If two items are failed, or one failed twice, a new application must be made for a re-test. A re-test may not be granted within one month of the failed test.
3 Bronze and Silver standards may be taken on the same occasion.
4 Assessors are responsible for arranging:
i suitable controllers to give each candidate a fair chance, and ii a scorer, to keep count of successes and errors.
5 The controller should be a player able to place slow and steady balls to the required targets, with required spin. Mistakes by the controller, or unlucky balls, or balls which are not appropriate to the required test skill, will not be counted against the candidate.
6 Assessors will rule on quality of performance appropriate to each test level. A warning and explanation should be given to any candidate who does not appear to have understood the precise requirements of any test.
A push shot is a return which is low, slow, and straight, with a trace of backspin.
7 Appropriate target areas are shown in the diagram on page 111. Since the aim of Proficiency Awards is to train players to maintain control of length and direction, the Assessor should require good consistency in these respects, but allow for difficulties caused by inconsistent 'feeding' from the controller, or difficult playing conditions. If the exchange becomes difficult, it is fairer to call a 'let', and re-start from the score already reached.
8 Marking of the table: A, B, C, D, are centre points of the four 'courts'. Target areas may be regarded as a 'notional' 18 in (c. 45 cm) square. They need not be marked out in full; for practical purposes, the markers in the diagram provide a sufficient check on the length and directional control of the returns.
9 Assessors should inform candidates of their decisions and notify results to the Awards Organizer on the blue assessment form (no. 6811) which is obtainable from him at the address given on page 105.

10 Bronze Awards may be assessed by: teachers; league officials; E.T.T.A. coaches or students.

11 Silver Awards must be assessed by E.T.T.A. coaches.

12 Gold Awards will only be assessed at formal sessions organized by the E.T.T.A. and must be approved by a Staff Coach or an E.T.T.A. Approved Instructor.

13 Parents may not assess their own children above Bronze level.

All enquiries should be addressed to The National Awards Organizer at the address given on p. 105.

TARGET AREAS

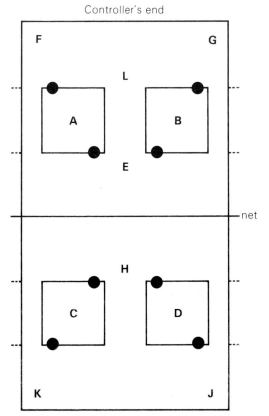

Controller's end

Candidate's end

Basic laws of table tennis

The following are extracts from the *Rules of the International Table Tennis Federation*

1 The table

The table shall be in surface rectangular, 2.74 m in length and 1.525 m in width; it shall be supported so that its upper surface, termed the 'playing surface', shall lie in a horizontal plane 760 mm above the floor. It shall be made of any material and shall yield a uniform bounce of not less than 220 mm and not more than 250 mm when a standard ball is dropped from a height of 305 mm above its surface. The playing surface shall be dark-coloured, preferably dark green, and matt, with a white line 20 mm broad along each edge. The lines at the 1.525 m edges, or ends, shall be termed 'end lines', and the lines at the 2.74 m edges, or sides, shall be termed 'side lines'. For doubles, the playing surface shall be divided into halves by a white line 3 mm broad, running parallel to the side lines, termed the 'centre line'. The centre line may, for convenience, be permanently marked in full length on the table and this in no way invalidates the table for singles play.

2 The net and its supports

The playing surface shall be divided into two 'courts' of equal size by a net running parallel to the end lines. The net, with its suspension, shall be 1.83 m in length; along its whole length its upper part shall be 152.5 mm above the playing surface and its lower part shall be close to the playing surface. It shall be suspended by a cord attached at each end to an upright post 152.5 mm high; the outside limits of each post shall be 152.55 mm outside the side line.

4 The racket

The racket may be of any size, shape or weight, but each side shall be uniformly dark-coloured and matt. The blade shall be of wood, continuous, of even thickness, flat and rigid. Any trimming or binding round the edge of the blade need not be of the same colour as either side but shall not be white, yellow or brightly reflecting. If a side of the blade used for striking the ball is covered, this covering, which shall extend over the whole striking surface, shall be either ordinary pimpled rubber, with pimples outwards, having a total thickness including adhesive of not more than 2 mm, or 'sandwich' rubber, consisting of a layer of cellular rubber surfaced by ordinary pimpled rubber, with pimples inwards or outwards, having a total thickness including adhesive of not more than 4 mm. If a side of the blade used for striking the ball is not covered the wood shall be dark-coloured, either naturally or by being stained, not painted, in such a way as not to alter the frictional characteristics of the surface. The part of the blade nearest the handle and gripped by the fingers may be covered with material such as cork for convenience of grip and is to be regarded as part of the handle. A side of the blade never used for striking the ball may be painted or covered with any material provided that the surface is uniformly dark-coloured and matt; a stroke with such a surface would, however, be illegal and result in a lost point. Minor variations of shade, due to wear or ageing of the surface, should not be regarded as infringing the requirement for uniformity, which is intended to prevent the use of basically different colours on a single side of the blade.

5 The order of play

In singles, the server shall first make a good service, the receiver shall then make a good return and thereafter server and receiver shall each alternately make a good return.

In doubles, the server shall first make a good service, the receiver shall then make a good return, the partner of the server shall then make a good return, and thereafter each player alternately in that sequence shall make a good return.

6 A good service

Service shall begin with the ball resting on the palm of the free hand, which must be stationary, open and flat, with the fingers together and the thumb free. The free hand, while in contact with the ball in service, shall at all times be above the level of the playing surface.

The server shall then project the ball upwards within 45 degrees of the vertical, by hand only

and without imparting spin, so that the ball
is visible at all times to the umpire and so that it
visibly leaves the palm.

As the ball is then visibly descending from the
height of its trajectory it shall be struck so that it
touch first the server's court and then, passing
directly over or around the net, touch the receiver's
court.

In doubles, the ball shall touch first the server's
right half-court or the centre-line on his side of
the net and then, passing over or around the net,
touch the receiver's right half-court or the centre
line on his side of the net.

At the moment of the impact, of the racket on
the ball in service, the ball shall be behind the
end-line of the server's court or an imaginary
extension thereof.

Strict observance of the prescribed method of
service may be waived where the umpire is
notified, before play begins, that compliance is
prevented by physical disability.

7 A good return

The ball having been served or returned in play
shall be struck so that it pass directly over or
around the net and touch directly the opponent's
court, provided that if the ball, having been served
or returned in play, return with its own impetus
over or around the net it may be struck while still
in play so that it touch directly the opponent's
court. If the ball, in passing over or around the
net, touch it or its supports it shall be considered
to have passed directly.

8 In play

The ball is in play from the moment at which it is
projected from the hand in service until:

a it has touched one court twice consecutively.

b it has, except in service, touched each court
alternately without having been struck with the
racket intermediately.

c it has been struck by a player more than once
consecutively.

d it has touched a player or anything he wears or
carries, except his racket or his racket hand
below the wrist.

114   **e** it has been volleyed.

f it has touched any object other than the net,

supports, or those referred to above.

g it has, in a doubles service, touched the left
half-court of the server or of the receiver.

h it has, in doubles, been struck by a player out of
proper sequence, except as provided in Law 15.

i it has, under the Expedite System, been
returned by thirteen successive good returns
of the receiving player or pair.

9 A let

The rally is a let:

a if the ball served, in passing over or around the
net, touch it or its supports, provided the service
be otherwise good or be volleyed by the
receiver, or his partner.

b if a service be delivered when the receiver or his
partner is not ready, provided always that a
player may not be deemed to be unready if he
or his partner attempt to strike at the ball.

c if, owing to an accident not within his control,
a player fail to make a good service or a good
return.

d if it be interrupted for correction of a mistake
in playing order or ends.

e if it be interrupted for application of the Expedite System.

10 A point

Except as provided in Law 9, a player shall lose a
point:

a if he fails to make a good service.

b if, a good service or a good return having been
made by his opponent, he fail to make a good
return.

c if he, or his racket or anything that he wears or
carries, touch the net or its supports while the
ball is in play.

d if he, or his racket, or anything that he wears or
carries, move the playing surface while the ball
is in play.

e if his free hand touch the playing surface while
the ball is in play.

f if, before the ball in play shall have passed over
the end lines or side lines not yet having touched
the playing surface on his side of the net since
being struck by his opponent, it come in
contact with him or anything he wears or carries.

g if he volley the ball.

h if, in doubles, he strike the ball out of proper sequence, except as provided in Law 15.

i if, under the Expedite System, his service and the twelve following strokes of the serving player or pair be returned by good returns of the receiving player or pair.

11 A game

A game shall be won by the player or pair first scoring 21 points, unless both players or pairs shall have scored 20 points, when the winner of the game shall be the player or pair first scoring 2 points more than the opposing player or pair.

13 The choice of ends and service

The choice of ends and the right to serve or receive first in a match shall be decided by toss. The winner of the toss may choose the right to serve or receive first and the loser shall then have the choice of ends and vice versa; the winner of the toss may, if he prefer it, require the loser to make first choice.

In doubles, the pair who have the right to serve the first five services in any game shall decide which partner shall do so. In the first game of a match the opposing pair shall then decide similarly which shall be the first receiver. In subsequent games the serving pair shall choose their first server and the first receiver will then be established automatically to correspond with the first server as provided in Law 14.

14 The change of ends and service

The player or pair who started at one end in a game shall start at the other in the immediately subsequent game, and so on until the end of the match. In the last possible game of the match the players or pairs shall change ends when first either player or pair reaches the score 10.

In singles, after five points, the receiver shall become the server and the server the receiver, and so on until the end of the game or the score 20–20, or until the introduction of the Expedite System.

In doubles, the first five services shall be delivered by the selected partner of the pair who **116** have the right to do so and shall be received by the appropriate partner of the opposing pair. The second five services shall be delivered by the receiver of the first five services and received by the partner of the first server. The third five services shall be delivered by the partner of the first server and received by the partner of the first receiver. The fourth five services shall be delivered by the partner of the first receiver and received by the first server. The fifth five services shall be delivered as the first five and so on in sequence until the end of the game or the score 20–20, or until the introduction of the Expedite System.

From the score 20–20, or if the game is being played under the Expedite System, the sequence of serving and receiving shall be the same but each player shall deliver only one service in turn until the end of the game.

The player or pair who served first in a game shall receive first in the immediately subsequent game, and so on until the end of the match. In the last possible game of a doubles match, the receiving pair shall alter its order of receiving when first either pair reaches the score 10.

In each game of a doubles match the initial order of receiving shall be opposite to that in the preceding game.

15 Out of order of ends, serving or receiving

If by mistake the players have not changed ends when ends should have been changed, they shall change ends as soon as the mistake is discovered, unless a game has been completed since the error, when the error shall be ignored.

If by mistake a player serve or receive out of his turn, play shall be interrupted as soon as the mistake is discovered and shall continue with that player serving or receiving who, according to the sequence established at the beginning of the match, should be server or receiver respectively at the score that has been reached.

In any circumstances, all points scored before the discovery of an error shall be reckoned.

16 Expedite system

If a game be unfinished fifteen minutes after it has begun, the rest of that game and the remaining games of the match shall proceed under the Expedite System. Thereafter, if the service and twelve following strokes of the serving player or pair be returned by good returns of the receiving player or pair, the server shall lose the point.

If the game is interrupted during a rally for the introduction of the Expedite System, play shall be re-started by service from the player who served for the rally that was interrupted; if the interruption occurs between rallies, play shall be re-started by service from the player who received first in the preceding rally. The Expedite System may be introduced at any earlier time, from the beginning of the match up to the end of fifteen minutes' play in any game, at the request of both players or pairs.

17 Definitions and interpretations

a The period during which the ball is in play shall be termed a 'rally'. A rally the result of which is not scored shall be termed a 'let', and a rally the result of which is scored shall be termed a 'point'.

b The player who first strikes the ball during a rally shall be termed the 'server', and the player who next strikes the ball shall be termed the 'receiver'.

c The 'racket hand' is the hand carrying the racket, and the 'free hand' is the hand not carrying the racket.

d 'Struck' means 'hit with the racket, carried in the racket hand, or with the racket hand below the wrist'. A stroke made with the hand alone, after dropping the racket, or by the racket after it has slipped or been thrown from the hand, is 'not good'.

e If the ball in play comes into contact with the racket or the racket hand below the wrist, not yet having touched the playing surface on one side of the net since last being struck on the other side, it shall be said to have been 'volleyed'.

f The 'playing surface' shall be regarded as including the top edges of the table, and a ball in play which strikes these latter is, therefore, 'good' and still in play; if it strikes the side of the table-top below the edge it becomes out of play and counts against the last striker.

g 'Around the net' means under or around the projection of the net and its supports outside the table, but not between the end of the net and the post.

h If a player, in attempting to serve, misses the
ball altogether he loses a point because the ball
is in play from the moment it is deliberately
projected from the hand.

Please Note:
In common with the rules of any other sport, the
laws of table tennis may be amended from time to
time by the governing committee, and players
would be well advised to keep up to date with
these changes.

The official magazine of the English Table
Tennis Association, *Table Tennis News*, contains
all the up-to-date information as well as many
other interesting items for the table tennis enthusi-
ast, and I thoroughly recommend all players to
read the monthly issues of the magazine, which can
be obtained from the headquarters of the
E.T.T.A. (see p. 10)

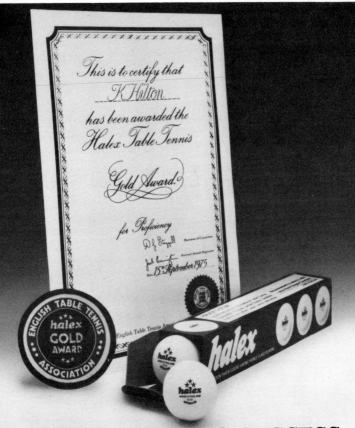

HALEX DOUBLES SUCCESS

HALEX 3 Star Table Tennis Balls have been officially selected for the 1977 World Championships.

The popularity of the Halex Proficiency Award Scheme introduced to help coaches to raise general playing standards has exceeded all expectations. Share in this success and improve your game by entering the Scheme.

Graded tests prepared by the English Table Tennis Association qualify for bronze, silver and gold awards.

Successful candidates receive Proficiency Certificates and attractive badges.

For full details apply to:—
Jack Carrington, National Awards Organiser.
71 Maplin Way, Thorpe Bay, Essex.

halex -the choice of champions

Index